The Effects of Social Security on Income and the Capital Stock

Michael R. Darby

The Effects of Social Security on Income and the Capital Stock

Michael R. Darby

American Enterprise Institute for Public Policy Research
Washington, D.C.

Michael R. Darby is professor of economics at the University of California, Los Angeles, and research associate at the National Bureau of Economic Research.

Library of Congress Cataloging in Publication Data

Darby, Michael R
    The effects of social security on income and the capital stock.

    Bibliography: p.
    1. Social security—United States.   2. Saving and investment—United States.   I. Title.
    HD7125.D37   368.4′00973   78-26424
    ISBN O-8447-3329-6

AEI Studies 227

Printed in the United States of America

To Margaret

CONTENTS

PREFACE

Martin Feldstein rekindled academic interest in social security with his seminal 1974 *Journal of Political Economy* article discussed at length in the text. This monograph grew like Topsy as the author tried to resolve questions raised by Feldstein's theoretical and empirical approaches. There were four main questions: (1) What happens when appropriate allowance is made for reduced dissaving by retirees which offsets the reduced saving by workers because of social security? (2) What happens when significant expected bequests are incorporated into the life-cycle saving model? (3) How are the results changed when alternative, more up-to-date consumption functions are substituted in the empirical analysis for that used by Feldstein? (4) How are effects on the saving–income ratio correctly translated into effects on real income and the capital stock in a long-run general equilibrium setting? These questions define the scope of the study.

Martin Feldstein, Milton Friedman, and I were involved in an extensive three-way correspondence that sharpened the questions just raised. Friedman then served as honest broker in letting Colin Campbell know that I was interested in doing just the sort of research that Campbell was responsible for funding through the American Enterprise Institute. Colin Campbell had gotten me into academic economics when I was an undergraduate at Dartmouth, and it was a pleasure to be involved with him again. His careful editing has contributed greatly to the readability and substance of this monograph. Valuable comments and data sources have been provided by many colleagues and friends, particularly Robert Barro, Michael Boskin, Stanley Engerman, Louis Esposito, Martin Feldstein, Michael Hurd, Laurence Kotlikoff, Alicia Munnell, Anthony Pellechio, Jeffrey Williamson, and members of the money workshops at the University of California, Los Angeles (UCLA), and the University of California,

Santa Barbara. The Foundation for Research in Economics and Education provided funding that supported the initial work on the subject. The final version was completed while the author was a visiting fellow at the Hoover Institution, Stanford University. This is not an official report of the NBER.

I was fortunate to be supported by three able research assistants, John Antel, Pamela Barnes, and Leslie Kent. They were persistent, diligent, and careful. No more could be asked. Henrietta Reason and Katherine Swan typed draft upon draft of the manuscript with unparalleled accuracy and efficiency. Unfortunately, no one but the author is left to blame for any remaining errors.

MICHAEL R. DARBY
Stanford, California
November 1977

1
Introduction and Summary

After a long period of neglect, the social security program is being reexamined on a wide front: equity, actuarial soundness, and economic impact. This monograph focuses on its economic effects and, in particular, its effects on income and the capital stock.

In a seminal study in the *Journal of Political Economy*, Martin Feldstein estimated that social security reduced U.S. saving and the capital stock by 38 percent.[1] In a climate of anxiety over a capital shortage, this estimate raised serious concern about the economic impact of social security.[2] This concern was expressed in several proposals, including one to change social security from a pay-as-you-go basis to a fully funded basis. The current study makes no attempt to evaluate these proposals. Instead, it focuses on evaluating the empirical and theoretical basis upon which the capital effects have been estimated and on improving them.

The social security program influences the aggregate levels of income and the capital stock in two ways: through its effect on the ratio of aggregate saving (or investment) to aggregate income, and through its effect on the supply of labor offered for employment. Generally, a reduction in either the saving–income ratio or the fraction of the population participating in the labor force will lower income and the capital stock.

Disagreements over the effects of social security concern primarily the estimated reduction in the saving–income ratio. The bulk

---

[1] Martin Feldstein, "Social Security, Induced Retirement, and Aggregate Capital Accumulation," *Journal of Political Economy*, vol. 82 (September/October 1974), pp. 905–26.

[2] A succinct review of the capital shortage literature is found in Robert Eisner, "Capital Shortage: Myth and Reality," *American Economic Review, Papers and Proceedings*, vol. 67 (February 1977), pp. 110–15.

1

of the work reported here is an examination of this issue. However, in Chapter 5, these effects are combined with labor supply changes in a model of long-run growth equilibrium.

The theoretical analysis of the effects of social security on the saving–income ratio has been made by Feldstein and others in terms of a model of the decisions people make about lifetime consumption, saving, and labor—with no expected bequests. This theoretical analysis is extended in Chapter 2 to include expected bequests. Such bequests arise not only out of concern for the welfare of heirs, but also because assets serve as a form of generalized insurance against contingencies.

The extended theoretical model in Chapter 2 suggests five ways in which social security can affect saving in relation to income. First, there is the dual effect of income-smoothing, which reduces aggregate saving, and of induced retirement, which increases aggregate saving. In this study, the net impact of these two offsetting effects is termed the Feldstein-Munnell effect after Martin Feldstein and Alicia Munnell who developed the concept. Second, social security may force people to buy life annuities which they would not otherwise buy. Because this reduces the risk of outliving any given amount of capital, the precautionary motive for expected bequests and saving is lessened. Third, however, the uncertainty in the amount of social security benefits that a person will receive tends to increase life-cycle saving. Fourth, saving also depends on the relationship between the real interest rate used by individuals in making their life-cycle decisions and the approximately 3.25 percent yield implicit in social security. If this real rate exceeded the implicit yield on social security, saving would increase. Finally, an induced reduction in the labor supply would tend to reduce both saving for bequests and income proportionately.

No unambiguous theoretical conclusions can be drawn about whether the social security program tends to increase or decrease the saving–income ratio. The extended model does suggest that analyses which concentrate exclusively on the Feldstein-Munnell effect may miss other important effects.

A factor that tends to reduce the size of all the effects of social security except those from induced changes in the labor supply is that, in part, social security does not change life-cycle income, but rather the labels applied to it. Old Age and Survivors Insurance (OASI) has replaced some public welfare financed by taxes and private income transfers from young workers to retired parents. The replacement of these transfers with social security benefits and taxes should have no effect on saving behavior.

2

The view that the zero-bequest life-cycle model does not tell the whole story about aggregate saving is explored further in Chapter 3. Actually, the whole idea of retirement is fairly modern. Chapter 3 examines whether saving in earlier years when people typically worked until they died conformed to the predictions of the zero-bequest life-cycle model. That model implies that the saving–income ratio increases with the ratio of expected retirement to expected working life. In fact, the saving–income ratio was at least as high from 1890 to 1930 as at present, and it tended to fall as the ratio of expected retirement to expected working life rose. This is contrary to the zero-bequest model and seems to suggest an important role for bequest saving. Indeed, the saving–income ratio from 1890 to 1930 was at least three to four times higher than can be explained by the zero-bequest model.

To test further whether the relative importance of life-cycle and bequest saving has changed in recent years, data on net worth from the 1967 Survey of Economic Opportunity (SEO) are also examined in Chapter 3. Total net worth by age was divided into a component held for life-cycle purposes and the remainder accumulated for expected bequests. The method of estimation used in this analysis tended to overestimate the portion held for life-cycle purposes, but these life-cycle assets were still only 13 to 29 percent of total assets, depending on the interest rate used. Once again, bequest saving appears to be empirically important.

The maximum possible Feldstein-Munnell effect was also calculated. This maximum effect occurs if net social security wealth replaces life-cycle assets dollar-for-dollar and there is no induced retirement. Using the cross-section data from the Survey of Economic Opportunity, this maximum reduction in total assets ranged (depending on the interest rate) from 12 to 23 percent of total assets inclusive of social security wealth. Similar calculations based on 1971 aggregate benefit data ranged from 11 to 21 percent. Feldstein's own estimate of net social security wealth was 25 percent at an interest rate corresponding to the above estimates of 21 and 23 percent. Because bequest assets and saving are large relative to life-cycle assets and saving, the potentially large percentage reduction in life-cycle assets and saving is only a small fraction of total assets and saving.

Direct estimates of the effects of social security on the saving–income ratio are included in Chapter 4. Previous efforts to estimate this effect using international cross-section data have been plagued with reverse causation. The fact that the saving–income ratio is negatively correlated with the size of the social security program may indicate that large social security programs either depress saving or are demanded when saving is low. The use of the U.S. time series data appears to be a more promising approach to estimating the effects on the saving–income ratio than the use of international cross-section data. Alicia Munnell, Martin Feldstein, and Robert Barro have produced estimates of the effects using time series data.

Munnell estimated that social security reduced private saving relative to income by about 5 percent, but her estimate was not statistically significant.

Feldstein estimated that social security reduced the private saving–income ratio by 38 percent, but his estimate is questionable. First, when we use Feldstein's concept of net social security wealth, which is statistically and theoretically superior to his concept of gross social security wealth, and delete an erroneous correction for social security effects on disposable income, the estimated reduction in the saving–income ratio is 26 percent. More important, his estimated effect was statistically significant only after the unemployment variable was deleted from his regression equation. Deleting the unemployment variable does not appear justified.

Barro has demonstrated the sensitivity of Feldstein's results to the unemployment variable and the period of estimation. Using Feldstein's social security wealth as well as a benefit-coverage variable, Barro has estimated that social security does not have a statistically significant effect on saving unless the unemployment variable (which is statistically significant) is deleted.

Chapter 4 includes regression results for four alternative social security scale variables: Feldstein's concepts of gross and net social security wealth, Barro's benefit-coverage variable, and OASI taxes. Using a refined consumer expenditure function derived from a permanent income model that explicitly allows for bequests, reductions (statistically significant only at the 0.20 level) of 25 to 30 percent in the saving–income ratio were estimated for 1929–1974 for three of the alternatives. No such reduction was found using Barro's variable. These estimated reductions in the saving–income ratio may be biased because the social security variables could serve as an indicator of whether or not there is a depression. It has been argued that consumption would be overestimated during the depression because the exhaustion of buffer stocks of liquid assets would cause a greater reduction in consumption than otherwise. Regressions run for 1947–1974 show no effect of social security on saving. It is concluded that the effect of social security on the saving–income ratio is still an open question. The estimated reduction of 25 to 30 percent in the saving–

income ratio is probably biased upward. The true reduction is probably closer to or less than 10 percent.

A wide range of estimated effects of social security on saving have been reported by researchers using apparently similar regression equations and the U.S. time series data. Taken as a whole, this evidence suggests that the saving–income ratio may have been reduced anywhere from 0 to 25 percent, although the range from 0 to 10 percent appears most probable. The labor supply reduction caused by social security apparently lies in the narrower range from 0 to 3 percent. Less research has been done on this magnitude, however.

Because the U.S. capital market is connected to the world capital market through international capital flows, the capital stock used in the United States (regardless of who owns it) should be distinguished from the capital stock owned by U.S. residents (regardless of where it is located). A corresponding distinction between output produced in the United States (net domestic product) and U.S. income (net national product) allows for the yield on net foreign capital holdings.

For the relevant range of interest rates, owned capital and income are likely to be reduced somewhat less in an open economy. Used capital and output would be reduced even less. The estimated reduction in owned capital is from 5 percent to 20 percent and used capital from 0 to 15 percent. The corresponding reductions in income and output range from 2 percent to 7 percent and from 0 to 4 percent, respectively.

2
A Model of the Effects of Social Security on the Saving–Income Ratio

This chapter discusses the two principal sources of saving in the economy—the accumulation of assets to finance retirement and the accumulation of assets to be bequeathed to one's heirs—and then examines how social security might affect them.

Zero-Bequest Model

The examination first focuses on how saving would occur in a world without bequests. This is the standard assumption in the model of saving over the life cycle developed by Modigliani, Brumberg, Ando, and others.[1] The unit of analysis is the individual, but this may be interpreted as a couple who marry at or before the beginning of their working life and die together at the end of retirement. Departures from this standard pattern will be considered in the analysis of cross-section data in Chapter 3.

---

[1] Some of the more important references are Franco Modigliani and Richard Brumberg, "Utility Analysis and the Consumption Function: An Interpretation of Cross-Section Data," in *Post Keynesian Economics*, ed. K.E. Kurihara (New Brunswick, N.J.: Rutgers University Press, 1954); Albert Ando and F. Modigliani, "The Life Cycle Hypothesis of Saving: Aggregate Implications and Tests," *American Economic Review*, vol. 53 (March 1963), pp. 55–84; F. Modigliani, "The Life Cycle Hypothesis of Saving, the Demand for Wealth, and the Supply of Capital," *Social Research*, vol. 33 (June 1966), pp. 160–217; David Cass and Menahem E. Yaari, "Individual Saving, Aggregate Capital Accumulation, and Efficient Growth," in *Essays on the Theory of Optimal Growth*, ed. Karl Shell (Cambridge, Mass.: MIT Press, 1967); James Tobin, "Life Cycle Saving and Balanced Growth," in *Ten Economic Studies in the Tradition of Irving Fisher*, William Fellner and others (New York: John Wiley and Sons, 1967); Gilbert R. Ghez and Gary S. Becker, *The Allocation of Time and Goods over the Life Cycle* (New York: National Bureau of Economic Research, 1975); and James J. Heckman, "A Life-Cycle Model of Earnings, Learning and Consumption," *Journal of Political Economy*, vol. 84 (August 1976), pp. S11–S44.

FIGURE 1

LIFE-CYCLE PATTERN OF LABOR EARNINGS AND CONSUMPTION
IN A ZERO-BEQUEST MODEL

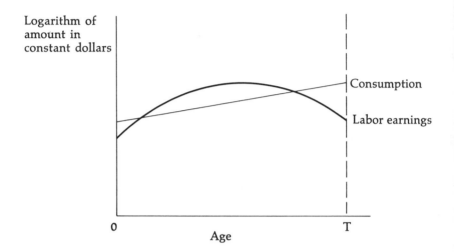

The life-cycle model is illustrated in Figure 1. On the horizontal axis, age is dated from the beginning of the individual's working life (age 0) to his death at age T. The vertical axis measures consumption and labor earnings in terms of the logarithm of real (inflation-corrected) dollars.[2] The curved line is the path of labor earnings over the life cycle. The humped shape reflects both variation in hours of work and wage rates.[3] Consumption of goods is drawn as a straight line, which implies a constant growth rate over the life cycle. Consumption will generally rise with age because, if a given amount is saved rather than consumed now, more goods can be purchased later with the principal and interest. Since future goods

---

[2] Such a logarithmic or ratio scale is convenient because variables growing at a constant proportional rate are depicted as straight lines.

[3] These factors could in turn be related to the life-cycle plan for investment in and depreciation of human capital. See, for example, Ghez and Becker, *The Allocation of Time and Goods over the Life Cycle*. The effects of social security on human capital plans will not be explicitly considered here, although they would appear to reinforce the effects of induced retirement discussed below. For simplicity, wage rates over the life cycle are assumed to be determined by age alone.

are cheaper now than current goods, more future goods will be purchased to equate the marginal utilities of future and present goods.[4] The rate of saving from labor income at each age is given by subtracting consumption from labor income. The individual's personal saving is found by adding the interest on accumulated past personal saving.

Figure 2 shows the corresponding pattern of an individual's asset holdings if bequests were zero. At first, assets are negative and falling with age because consumption exceeds labor income and interest must be paid on the negative assets (borrowings). Later, assets rise as labor earnings exceed consumption sufficiently to pay both interest and principal on the outstanding debt and to begin to build a fund of assets to finance excess of consumption over labor earnings in old age. The individual dissaves in his youth and to a much greater extent in his old age. The individual's personal dissaving just offsets his personal saving over his lifetime—he begins his working life with nothing and dies with nothing. His saving serves in effect to shift labor earnings from high earning years. This is referred to as "income smoothing."

Although each individual has zero net saving over his lifetime, this life-cycle saving can provide positive aggregate saving each year for the economy as a whole. This is because the amount of saving done by each age group, or cohort, depends on the average life-cycle labor earnings per individual and on the number of individuals. In an economy characterized by growth in population and productivity (so long as the youthful dissaving is small relative to saving for and dissaving during old age), the savers will be richer and more numerous than the dissavers.[5]

An alternative way of describing the same process is in terms of saving as accumulation of assets. As productivity and labor earnings grow, the typical life-cycle pattern of assets for each succeeding cohort grows in proportion. Income and consumption move up together and so does the amount of income smoothing required.

---

[4] Formally, a first-order condition for optimality requires that:

$$\frac{\text{marginal utility of consumption at } t}{\text{marginal utility of consumption at } t + \tau} = (1 + r)^{\tau},$$

where r is the (assumed positive) difference between the real rate of interest and the rate of pure time preference. In order for the numerator to exceed the denominator, consumption must be less in t than in $t + \tau$. If the utility function is homothetic in consumption and bequests, and if these and leisure are separable, consumption will indeed grow at a constant rate. There is no a priori reason nor much empirical evidence to depart from the straight-line approximation.
[5] If the growth rate were high enough, however, the dissaving of the young would predominate and aggregate saving would be negative. The complications of youthful dissaving are generally neglected in the literature.

FIGURE 2

LIFE-CYCLE PATTERN OF AN INDIVIDUAL'S TOTAL ASSETS
IN A ZERO-BEQUEST MODEL

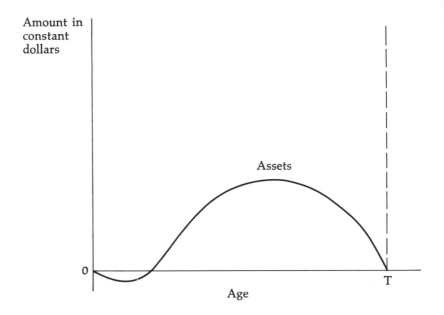

Furthermore, each succeeding cohort is more numerous than the preceding. As a result, total assets for the economy will grow by the sum of the growth rates of population and productivity—that is, by the growth rate of real income. Life-cycle saving is the product of the growth rate of real income and the total amount of assets held by all individuals for income smoothing. Aggregate life-cycle saving thus depends on the mismatch between the life-cycle pattern of labor income and consumption. Factors that decrease this mismatch in old age decrease the amount of assets held for income smoothing and thus the aggregate amount of life-cycle saving.

Positive-Bequest Model

Figure 3 depicts the pattern of asset holdings for a typical individual on the assumption that positive bequests are left at the end of life and inheritances are received throughout life. In this case, aggregate personal saving will reflect both (1) variations in the rate of saving

FIGURE 3

Life-Cycle Pattern of an Individual's Total Assets in a Positive-Bequest Model

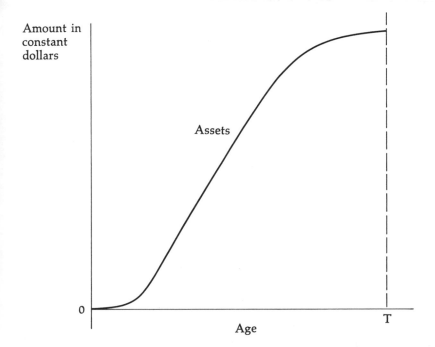

by age as in the simple zero-bequest model of Figure 1 and (2) any accumulation of funds for bequests at a faster rate than inheritances are received. Aggregate saving for bequests is the product of the growth rate of real income and the total amount of assets held by all individuals in anticipation of bequests. Income will be increased in the aggregate by the real interest rate times the assets held for bequest assets. This increased income finances both bequest saving and (if the real interest rate exceeds the growth rate of real income) a higher level of lifetime consumption.[6]

---

[6] As will be seen below, a full analysis is complicated by the fact that an increase in saving relative to income will generally result in higher total income, higher wages, and lower interest rates. Higher wages will tend to increase the "life-cycle" portion of aggregate saving by exaggerating the mismatch between labor income and consumption. Lower interest rates will imply less steep life-cycle growth in consumption and hence less aggregate life-cycle saving. These two second-round (or general equilibrium) effects need not precisely cancel out and could reinforce or partially offset the increase in saving because of accumulation of assets for bequests.

Many economists have assumed that the bequest motive for saving is unimportant. Transfers of assets to one's children have often been dismissed as irrational because on average each generation in a growing economy is better off than the last generation, and bequests would make the younger generations even wealthier relative to the older generation. There is, however, a rational basis for bequests to younger generations. At compound interest, a current sacrifice of consumption can provide much more consumption in the future. Thus, parents may rationally decide to forego some consumption in order to obtain more consumption for their children.

The bequest motive is closely related to the precautionary motive for holding assets. Uncertainties about length of life, state of health, and other "rainy days" can be met either by purchasing insurance (such as life insurance and major medical insurance) or by holding assets that can be used in any emergency. The costs of administration, adverse selection, and moral hazard may make insurance unattractive relative to assets that may eventually be bequeathed to one's children. The typical pattern, in which persons receive in middle age bequests that supplement their own retirement savings, fulfills the precautionary needs of an ongoing family and are a source of saving in the economy.

The precautionary motive can be viewed as supplementary to the bequest motive—or the bequest motive as supplementary to the precautionary motive. Both motives are involved in choosing a life-cycle consumption plan that does not completely exhaust expected income over the life cycle.

Effects of Social Security on the Saving–Income Ratio

Although the primary focus of this paper is the effect of social security on saving, as a practical matter it is better to examine the effects of social security on consumption rather than on saving because the effects on consumption are more directly observable. Saving is the difference between income and consumption. If social security reduces saving relative to income, it must increase consumption.

Old Age and Survivors Insurance might alter a person's consumption through four different channels: through induced early retirement and other changes in hours worked, through the differences in the present value of benefits and taxes, through changes in the precautionary demand for assets, and through changes in interest rates and wage rates.

Induced Retirement Effects. The social security program may cause changes in the amount of work a person does because of the earnings test and the payroll tax. The social security benefit of a retired worker aged sixty-two to seventy-one is reduced $1 for every additional $2 earned (until the benefit is completely exhausted) for any earnings over a given amount. In 1977 this amount was $250 a month or $3,000 a year for persons retiring at age sixty-five through seventy-one. This is equivalent to a marginal tax rate of 50 percent, and more than that if payroll and income taxes are taken into account. Some retirees earn just up to the maximum allowed without loss of benefits, while others do not work at all because of the fixed costs of working and reduced part-time wages. On the other hand, workers with relatively high wages may find it worthwhile to forego the retirement benefit entirely.

The current social security payroll tax (excluding medicare) of 9.9 percent—4.95 percent on both the employer and the employee—reduces a person's effective (after-tax) wage rate by a substantial amount. For example, if the employee's marginal income tax rate is 22 percent, and the payroll tax rate is 9.9 percent, his effective tax rate is increased from 22 percent to 30.6 percent by the payroll tax. The effective tax rate does not increase by the full 9.9 percent payroll tax rate because the tax on the employer is exempt from income tax. The estimated 30.6 percent tax rate is based on the worker's gross wage rather than the reported (after-employer-tax) wage. These high taxes on earnings may reduce hours worked before a person retires, but they need not have this effect because of off-setting wealth and substitution effects.

The lifetime paths of earnings and consumption of a typical individual before and after social security are shown in Figure 4. The solid lines show the earnings and consumption with social security, and the broken lines show them in the absence of social security. (Social security benefits are treated here as labor income while social security taxes are deducted from labor income.) It is assumed in Figure 4 that the individual retires at age R because of the earnings test.

The assumption in Figure 4 is that the net present value of social security taxes and benefits are equal at age 0, the beginning of a person's working life. This implies that the sum of the growth rates of population and productivity equal the real interest rate. Under these conditions, the worker who chooses to retire at age R loses no wealth directly. However, the involuntary nature of the social security system in which taxes must be paid and benefits are

13

FIGURE 4

THE EFFECT OF SOCIAL SECURITY ON THE LIFE-CYCLE PATTERN OF
LABOR EARNINGS AND CONSUMPTION WITH RETIREMENT INDUCED

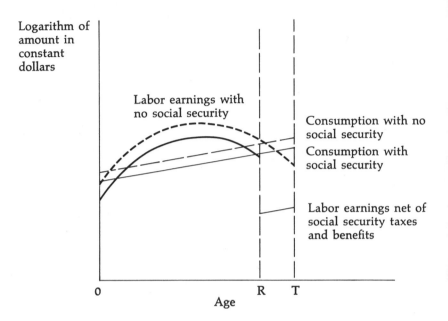

conditional on retirement causes people to retire earlier and more fully than they otherwise would have. They would prefer to continue working if they could receive the benefits that their past taxes "purchased." Without retiring, this is not possible. As a result, the net effect of social security is to induce persons to withdraw from the labor force after age R and to save more before age R in order to shift some of their labor earnings to old age. Thus, lifetime earnings and consumption fall.

Figure 4 shows labor earnings reduced by the payroll tax up to age R. At age R, labor earnings drop sharply because of the earnings test, and this drop is only partially compensated for by social security benefits. The amount of consumption that must be financed by life-cycle saving is greater with social security than without social security, so life-cycle saving is increased. With social security, a bigger fund of assets is accumulated to be dissaved during old age. For a given growth rate of real income, the larger the total amount of assets in the economy is, the larger total saving is.

FIGURE 5

The Effect of Social Security on the Life-Cycle Pattern of Labor Earnings and Consumption with Retirement Unaffected

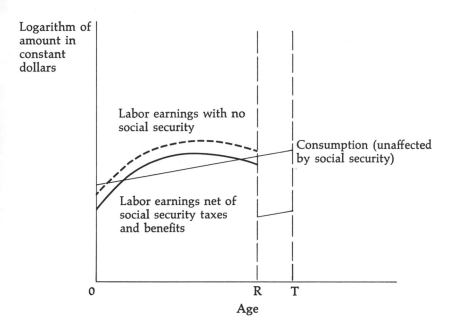

Figure 5 is based on the same assumptions as Figure 4 with one exception: it is assumed that the individual would retire at age R even in the absence of social security. Social security taxes and benefits are assumed not to change his lifetime wealth, so his consumption will be unaffected by social security. His after-tax earnings are reduced before age R, and social security benefits provide earnings between ages R and T. The typical individual now pays social security taxes instead of saving to accumulate a fund to finance the retirement consumption that will be financed by social security benefits. Therefore, total assets in the economy and aggregate saving are reduced.

There are two extreme cases. If the individual would not otherwise retire, the life-cycle patterns of income and consumption match less well under social security,[7] so a larger fund of assets is required to finance old age and saving is increased. If the individual would have retired at age R anyway, then social security reduces the mis-

---

[7] Unless earnings in old age would fall below the social security benefit.

15

match between income and consumption and aggregate saving is reduced. In the important intermediate case, in which the individual would retire between age R and age T, aggregate saving could be increased or decreased.

This analysis was developed by Martin Feldstein and Alicia Munnell for a zero-bequest life-cycle model.[8] They have concluded that the net effect on aggregate saving of income transfers from young to old and of induced retirement is ambiguous as a matter of theory. The empirical importance of these induced changes in the demand for assets through the life cycle will be considered in later chapters, but it is illuminating to consider the analysis a bit further here.

Consider the case of the individual who would have retired at age R anyway. If social security is actuarially fair (that is, if the expected net present values of benefits and taxes are equal), the individual will experience no change in his net wealth and no reason to change his consumption pattern.[9] If this were true for all individuals, even though aggregate consumption and labor input would be unaffected, aggregate saving would fall. The apparent paradox is resolved by noting that total income will fall by the interest rate times the reduction in the desired asset (or capital) stock. Since social security can be actuarially fair in a steady-state only if the real interest rate equals the growth rate of total income and the capital stock, the reduction in saving is just the amount required for the reduced capital stock to grow at the same rate as before. Although income, saving, and the capital stock are reduced, no individual reduces his consumption and, in addition, the generations alive at the beginning of the program can consume the excess capital stock.[10] This analysis provides little support for concern over a reduction in saving on welfare grounds, although some of the effects omitted from the analysis may be questioned as well as some of the implicit assumptions.[11]

---

[8] Martin Feldstein, "Social Security, Induced Retirement, and Aggregate Capital Accumulation," *Journal of Political Economy*, vol. 82 (September/October 1974), pp. 905–26; and Alicia H. Munnell, *The Effect of Social Security on Personal Saving* (Cambridge, Mass.: Ballinger Publishing Co., 1974).

[9] This is the case discussed in Feldstein, "Social Security, Induced Retirement, and Aggregate Capital Accumulation," pp. 908–09.

[10] Reference should be made here to three articles by Paul A. Samuelson: "An Exact Consumption-Loan Model of Interest with or without the Social Contrivance of Money," *Journal of Political Economy*, vol. 66 (December 1958), pp. 467–82; "The Optimal Growth Rate for Population," *International Economic Review*, vol. 16 (October 1975), pp. 531–38, and "Optimal Social Security in a Life-Cycle Growth Model," *International Economic Review*, vol. 16 (October 1975), pp. 539–44.

[11] Several of these assumptions are discussed below.

Regarding the bequest portion of aggregate saving, induced retirement would reduce saving—the opposite of the effect of induced retirement in the Feldstein-Munnell analysis. Earlier retirement would reduce the wealth a person has—whether allocated to lifetime consumption or to bequests. If, over the life cycle, a fraction of income is devoted to bequests, the reduced income would result in a more or less proportionate fall in consumption, bequests, and saving for bequests. If there were no (or negligible) life-cycle saving, the saving–income ratio would be unchanged if the fall in consumption were proportionate to the fall in the wealth value of labor earnings.[12] A smaller (larger) fall in consumption would cause the saving–income ratio to rise (fall).

Unless one makes special assumptions, there is no presumption about whether the effect of social security on induced retirement will increase, decrease, or leave unchanged the saving–income ratio. However, later when empirical estimates of the effects of social security on saving for given income levels are considered, an adjustment will be made for the fall in income resulting from the induced fall in labor supply.

Effects on Present Value of Benefits and Taxes. The previous discussion assumed that lifetime command over goods was altered only through induced changes in labor supply. This requires that the social security system be actuarially fair in the sense that at the beginning of the working life (age 0 in Figure 4) the net present values of expected taxes and benefits are equal. With a constant payroll tax rate and benefit replacement ratio,[13] per capita benefits will grow at the growth rate of real income. If the real interest rate used in discounting these benefits equals the growth rate of real income, the system will be actuarially fair because benefits will grow as fast as would a similar investment in real capital.

If, instead, the appropriate real interest rate is greater than the growth of real income—say, 10 percent as compared with 3.25 percent a year—then an involuntary social security program involves a net decrease in the wealth value of life-cycle labor income.[14] Such a

---

[12] This assumes that the real interest rate used in discounting future consumption and labor income is equal to growth rate of effective labor units (and real income) as required for actuarially fair social security in the steady state.

[13] The benefit replacement ratio is the ratio of a retiree's benefit to his earnings in the year before retirement.

[14] The fact that social security may produce a deadweight wealth loss in the steady-state pattern of taxes and benefits provides the possibility of ending the system so that everyone now living is made better off. Although benefits of some people now living would be paid by the yet unborn if the system con-

reduction in wealth would cause the desired levels of both consumption and bequests to fall. The fall in consumption of each individual would increase aggregate saving, but this increase is less in the presence of positive bequests than it would be if consumption was reduced by the full reduction in wealth. Precisely opposite effects would occur were the growth rate of real income to exceed the real interest rate, but this case is unlikely on both empirical and theoretical grounds.[15]

Precautionary Effects. The precautionary motive for holding assets is related to the bequest motive because the value of the potential use of assets in emergencies reduces the cost of bequests. The social security program in effect forces individuals to buy life annuities—not to mention health and other insurance. The annuities might be attractively priced compared with those available in the private market, where adverse selection might increase the cost. Nevertheless, the social security system provides people with annuities worth a certain amount, given their work history and marital status, and no more or less can be purchased.

Except for those who would otherwise purchase an equal amount of life annuities in the private insurance market, this forced purchase of a life annuity probably decreases the desired level of bequests. For most people, because social security reduces the danger of outliving one's income, assets for planned bequests lose some of their value as a reserve for emergencies.

On the other hand, since the social security benefits "purchased" with present taxes are uncertain,[16] individuals may save more during their working years and then dissave more during their retirement than would be the case if benefits were certain. The higher saving during working years represents a fall in consumption associated with a fall in expected wealth. Consumption then would rise during retirement years as higher-than-expected benefits are received. The net effect here is to increase the life-cycle portion of saving.

---

tinues, the resulting losses to younger workers may be great enough to pay off those nearing retirement and forego taxation of future generations. Edgar K. Browning neglected this and other losses when he argued that the social security program could not be ended because of the loss to those currently living; see Browning, "Social Insurance and Intergenerational Transfers," *Journal of Law and Economics*, vol. 16 (October 1973), pp. 215–37.

[15] See Earl A. Thompson, "Debt Instruments in Both Macroeconomic Theory and Capital Theory," *American Economic Review*, vol. 57 (December 1967), pp. 1196–1210.

[16] There is no legally vested interest in social security, for example.

Interest and Wage Rate Effects. The discussion so far has considered the possibilities of significant changes—up or down—in the saving–income ratio on the assumption that the real rate of interest and the real wage rates are fixed. In the neoclassical growth model of a closed economy, this does not make sense unless the elasticity of substitution between capital and labor is nearly infinite. However, for a relatively open economy such as the United States, real interest rates and wages may be determined in the world markets. If so, a reduction in saving in the United States would cause a decrease in net U.S. investment abroad.

It may be objected that the U.S. economy is either too large or too closed to be characterized as a small open economy only trivially affecting the world interest and wage rates. If this is so, a fall in the saving–income ratio would be expected to reduce the capital–labor ratio and the real wage rate and increase the interest rate. This would lead to further ambiguous, but presumably small, changes in the saving–income ratio. No attempt to analyze these second-order effects is made here.

Alternatives to Social Security. It should not be forgotten that the social security program in part replaces intergenerational transfers from young workers to retired parents and elderly welfare recipients that would otherwise take place. To the extent that it does, there would be no effect on an individual's life-cycle pattern of income or saving. Robert Barro has argued that parents would adjust their saving and bequests to offset the burden of social security taxes on future generations.[17] In an actuarially fair system, this burden does not exist unless it is presumed that the social security program will eventually end.

Summary

The social security system may affect the saving–income ratio through its effects on either the life-cycle demand for assets or the accumulation of assets for bequests.

The life-cycle portion of aggregate saving may be reduced if the match between income and consumption becomes closer because of the income-shifting and induced-retirement aspects of the social security program—the Feldstein-Munnell effect. On the other hand, if the real interest rate exceeds the growth rate of real income, the shift of income to retirement years through the social security system

---

[17] Robert J. Barro, "Are Government Bonds Net Wealth?" *Journal of Political Economy*, vol. 82 (November/December 1974), pp. 1095–1117.

will increase saving because of the lower wealth value of life-cycle earnings. Also, the uncertain nature of social security benefits may increase saving by decreasing consumption in the working years and increasing consumption during retirement.

The bequest portion of saving would be reduced by the social security system more or less in proportion to the induced reduction in the supply of labor. If there were no other effects, the saving–income ratio would be more or less unchanged. On the other hand, the saving–income ratio would tend to fall further because the precautionary function of expected bequests would be partially satisfied by social security.

Although the bequest portion of aggregate saving is expected to fall more than in proportion to income, it is not known whether the life-cycle portion will rise or fall either in absolute terms or relative to income. Thus, the broader analysis of possible effects of the social security system does not alter Feldstein's conclusion: "As is so often the case, a theoretical analysis can illuminate the ways in which a public policy affects individual behavior, but it cannot yield an estimate of the magnitude of the effect nor even an unambiguous conclusion about its sign. For this we must turn to an empirical investigation."[18] This is the subject of Chapters 3 and 4.

---

[18] Feldstein, "Social Security, Induced Retirement, and Aggregate Capital Accumulation," p. 910.

3

The Relative Importance of Intergenerational Transfers and Life-Cycle Motivations for Aggregate Saving

Recent empirical investigations of the effects of social security on saving have been based on life-cycle models with zero bequests.[1] This implicitly assumes that the bequest portion of aggregate saving is unimportant. This chapter attempts to analyze whether this assumption is correct.

Two different approaches will be used to determine the relative importance of the life-cycle and bequest portions of aggregate saving. The first approach examines the effect on the aggregate private saving rate of the rise in retirement during the 1890–1930 period. In the life-cycle model, this should have caused a substantial rise in the saving–income ratio. In fact, the saving–income ratio tended to decline during this period and was three to four times larger than could be explained by the life-cycle model.

The second approach is to estimate the portion of total assets held for life-cycle as opposed to bequest purposes. Estimates for 1970 of the amount of assets that would yield an annuity stream equivalent to social security benefits anticipated by people twenty years of age and older range downward from $943 billion—less than half of Feldstein's estimate for the same year. Also, an examination of cross-section survey data showed that the life-cycle demand for assets accounted for only 13 to 29 percent of total assets.

---

[1] Reference is made here particularly to Martin Feldstein, "Social Security, Induced Retirement, and Aggregate Capital Accumulation," *Journal of Political Economy*, vol. 82 (September/October 1974), pp. 905–26; Alicia H. Munnell, *The Effect of Social Security on Personal Saving* (Cambridge, Mass.: Ballinger Publishing Co., 1974); and their numerous follow-up papers, as well as to an interesting unpublished study by Laurence J. Kotlikoff, Christopher Chamby, and Anthony Pellechio, "Social Security and Private Wealth Accumulation," Harvard University, Department of Economics, November 1976.

The statistical data examined in this chapter raise serious questions about the empirical usefulness of the zero-bequest life-cycle model for analyzing aggregate saving and the effects of social security on the saving–income ratio. Even substantial changes in the small life-cycle portion of saving would have a relatively minor effect on total saving.

Effects of the Rise in Retirement on the Saving–Income Ratio, 1890–1929

The life-cycle model is based upon a pattern of working years followed by retirement years, even though this pattern is largely a twentieth century phenomenon. In previous centuries, a typical pattern would be a working life terminated by a short illness and death. If life-cycle saving is an important source of aggregate saving, the rise in retirement since the end of the nineteenth century should have caused a substantial increase in the saving–income ratio.

In 1890, the earliest year for which reliable data are available, 74 percent of the male population aged sixty-five and older were in the labor force. By 1930, the last census before social security was introduced, only about 58 percent of that population participated in the labor force, as shown in Table 1. At the same time that labor force participation was dropping among the elderly, the probability that a twenty-year-old worker would live to age sixty-five rose from about 0.41 to 0.60. The combined effect of these two forces was to increase substantially the length of time a typical worker could expect to spend in retirement.

Table 2 shows the expected years of remaining life and the expected years of retirement of males aged twenty based on life tables and labor force participation rates for the census years 1890–1930. In this table, retirement is defined as nonparticipation in the labor force by a person sixty-five years or older. Essentially the same pattern is shown for retirement defined as nonparticipation by a person aged sixty years or older. Column (3) gives the ratio of expected retirement to expected life. In the life-cycle model, this is an index of the fraction of a worker's income to be saved for retirement. This ratio increased from 3.8 percent in 1890 to 6.3 percent in 1930, an increase of some two-thirds.

Decade averages were computed for the saving–income ratio in order to smooth out short-run fluctuations caused by the business cycle and other transient phenomena. A variety of definitions of saving and income might be used, of which the most relevant is the ratio of private saving to private income. This definition encompasses

TABLE 1

LABOR FORCE PARTICIPATION OF MALE POPULATION SIXTY-FIVE YEARS
AND OLDER AND PROBABILITY OF A TWENTY-YEAR-OLD WORKER
LIVING TO AGE SIXTY-FIVE, 1890–1930

Year	Percent of Male Population 65 and Older in Labor Force (1)	Probability of 20-Year-Old Male Living to Age 65 (2)
1890	73.9	0.41
1900	68.3	0.51
1910	58.1	0.52
1920	60.1	0.60
1930	58.3	0.60

SOURCES: Column (1)—Clarence D. Long, *The Labor Force under Changing Income and Employment*, National Bureau of Economic Research, General Series 65 (Princeton, N.J.: Princeton University Press, 1958), Table A.2. Column (2)— for 1900–1930, computed from Thomas N.E. Greville, *United States Life Tables and Actuarial Tables 1939–1941* (Washington, D.C.: U.S. Government Printing Office, 1946), Table J, p. 11; for 1890, computed from U.S. Bureau of the Census, *1890 Census, Vital Statistics*, vol. 4, pt. 1, Table 10, p. 862.

TABLE 2

EXPECTED REMAINING LIFE AND EXPECTED RETIREMENT
OF TWENTY-YEAR-OLD MALES, 1890–1930

Year	Expected Life (years) (1)	Expected Retirement (years) (2)	Ratio of Expected Retirement to Expected Life (percent) (3)
1890	37.08	1.424	3.8
1900	42.19	1.853	4.4
1910	42.71	2.412	5.6
1920	45.60	2.893	6.3
1930	46.02	2.907	6.3

NOTE: Retirement is defined as nonparticipation in the labor force by a person sixty-five years or older.

SOURCES: For column (1), see sources for Table 1, column (2). For column (2), see sources for Table 1, columns (1) and (2). Column (3) = column (2) ÷ column (1).

all income received or accruing to private individuals—including un-distributed corporate profits—and thus corresponds to the rational behavior posited by the life-cycle model much more closely than disposable personal income. Statistical analysis has shown that since World War II private income has a closer relationship to consumption and saving than disposable personal income.[2] Private saving is the portion of this income not consumed or, in other words, the sum of net investment, net exports, and the government deficit.

Estimates of the ratio of private saving to private income by decades—depicted in column (1) of Table 3—show no trend. It is not certain how rapidly changes in mortality and retirement patterns would affect individual consumption-saving behavior. The data on the ratio of expected retirement to expected life, on the other hand, show a strong upward trend. In Figure 6, averages of the values of the retirement–life ratio at each end of the decades are compared with the saving–private income ratio. Essentially the same picture would be obtained if it were assumed that expectations lag or lead actual events. Figure 6 shows that there is no relation between the upward-trended retirement–life ratio and the untrended saving–income ratio. Although there is too little data for fancy statistical tests, the correlation is not only insignificant but also of the wrong (negative) sign.

If life-cycle motivations are an important source of aggregate saving, the saving–income ratio should have risen sharply as the retirement–life ratio rose. A possible explanation of why the data do not fulfill that expectation is that the definitions of saving or income are defective. A number of alternative definitions were considered with essentially the same results. Several alternatives are presented in Table 3.

Paul David and John Scadding have argued that the personal saving behavior of households is affected by government—as well as corporate—spending and saving.[3] They recommend using the gross private saving ratio (gross private saving to gross national product). In their estimates of the gross private saving ratio, they treat purchases of consumers' durable goods as part of gross investment and make a corresponding adjustment to gross national product for the yield on these goods. It was not feasible to do that in the estimates here. Column (2) of Table 3 shows the ratio of private saving plus

[2] See Michael R. Darby, "The Consumer Expenditure Function," *Explorations in Economic Research*, vol. 4 (Winter/Spring 1977–1978), pp. 645–74.

[3] Paul A. David and John L. Scadding, "Private Savings: Ultrarationality, Aggregation, and 'Denison's Law,'" *Journal of Political Economy*, vol. 82 (March/April 1974), pp. 225–49.

TABLE 3

Saving–Income Ratios, 1890–1929

Decade	Ratio of Private Saving to Private Income (1)	Ratio of Gross Private Saving to Gross National Product (2)	Ratio of Private Saving Minus the Government Deficit to Private Income Minus the Government Deficit (3)
1890–1899	0.129	0.210	0.122
1900–1909	0.123	0.198	0.117
1910–1919	0.153	0.231	0.087
1920–1929	0.094	0.169	0.094

Sources: Computations by the author based on data in: John W. Kendrick, *Productivity Trends in the United States*, National Bureau of Economic Research, General Series 71 (Princeton, N.J.: Princeton University Press, 1961); U.S. Bureau of Economic Analysis, *Long Term Economic Growth 1860–1970* (Washington, D.C.: U.S. Government Printing Office, 1973); U.S. Bureau of the Census, *Historical Statistics of the United States, Colonial Times to 1957* (Washington, D.C.: U.S. Government Printing Office, 1960); U.S. Bureau of the Census, *Historical Statistics of United States, Colonial Times to 1970*, 2 vols. (Washington, D.C.: U.S. Government Printing Office, 1975); U.S. Bureau of the Census, *1890 Census*, vol. 15, p. 77.

capital consumption allowances to gross national product. This ratio has the same trendless pattern—and an insignificant negative correlation with the expected retirement–life ratio—as the ratio of private saving to private income.

At least since David Ricardo, a large number of economists, and recently Robert Barro and Levis Kochin, have argued that government deficits will not reduce and surpluses will not augment the amount of saving available to finance private investment.[4] The basic idea is that, when there is a budget deficit, individuals will deduct from their current income the present value of the future taxes required to service the increased issue of government bonds. As a result, private saving will increase by just enough to finance the increased bond issues. Similarly, private saving would contract were the government to run a surplus. If this point of view is correct, private income and saving are overstated by the failure to deduct the tax liability corresponding to the government deficit.

[4] Robert J. Barro, "Are Government Bonds Net Wealth?" *Journal of Political Economy*, vol. 82 (November/December 1974), pp. 1095–1117; Levis A. Kochin, "Are Future Taxes Anticipated by Consumers?" *Journal of Money, Credit, and Banking*, vol. 6 (August 1974), pp. 385–94.

FIGURE 6

SAVING-INCOME RATIO VERSUS EXPECTED RETIREMENT–EXPECTED LIFE RATIO, 1890–1929

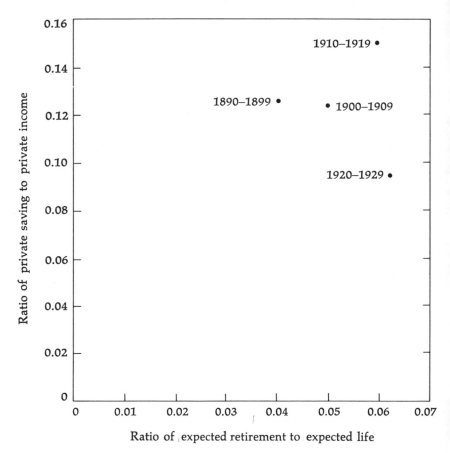

Column (3) of Table 3 presents the saving–income ratio with the amount of the government deficit subtracted from both saving and income. As the proponents of this point of view claim, adjusting for the World War I deficits and postwar surpluses results in a more stable saving–income ratio. Apparently, the assumption that the future taxes associated with deficits are only partially anticipated would result in an even more stable ratio. The ratio as computed has a slight negative trend—the opposite of that predicted by the life-cycle model.

The fact that the major change that has occurred in retirement patterns has no effect on the saving–income ratio appears to show that life-cycle motivations are a much less important source of aggregate saving than most persons have thought; this lack of effect may also result from some fortuitously offsetting forces. Possible examples of such offsetting forces are: increases in wealth, shifts in the population distribution, changes in the growth rate of real income, and reduction in economic uncertainty. The first two possibilities do not seem promising. It is usually thought that increases in wealth, if anything, increase the saving–income ratio. They would reinforce, but not offset, the effect of increased retirement on the saving–income ratio. The average age of the population did rise gradually over this period; for example, 3.85 percent of the male population was sixty-five or older in 1890 compared with 5.35 percent in 1930. But this aging is part and parcel of the increase in expected retirement relative to expected life which, as has been stated, has the effect of increasing aggregate saving relative to income in the life-cycle model.

The growth rate of real income is important in the life-cycle model because higher growth rates would imply that young savers are more numerous or wealthy than older dissavers. There was a downward trend in the growth rate of the real gross national product (GNP) over the four decades—from 4.3 percent in 1890–1899 to 4.2 percent, 2.3 percent, and then 3.4 percent in 1920–1929.[5] The 21 percent decline in the growth rate of real GNP from the 1890s to the 1920s would no more than partially offset the more than 50 percent increase in the ratio of expected retirement to expected life. The interactions of growth rates and the retirement–life ratio are complex, depending on the interest rate and on the precise life-cycle shape of income and consumption. However, calculations based on certain simplifying assumptions can be made using a formula developed by Modigliani.[6] Using the average expected retirement and expected remaining life of a twenty-year-old male for the 1890s and 1920s and the corresponding growth rates of 4.3 percent and 3.4 percent,

[5] These growth rates are for the Kendrick data from the year before the beginning of each decade to the last year in the decade; see John W. Kendrick, *Productivity Trends in the United States,* National Bureau of Economic Research, General Series 71 (Princeton, N.J.: Princeton University Press, 1961).

[6] Franco Modigliani, "The Life Cycle Hypothesis of Saving, the Demand for Wealth, and the Supply of Capital," *Social Research,* vol. 33 (June 1966), p. 169. It is assumed that earnings are constant over the working life, that consumption is constant over the whole life, and that the rate of return is zero. The formula given was derived strictly for growth because of population growth, which differs trivially in value from the formula for growth because of productivity growth.

Modigliani's formula predicts that aggregate (life-cycle) saving was 2.8 percent of income in the 1890s and 3.6 percent in the 1920s, a net increase of 0.8 of a percentage point or 29 percent. However, even with Modigliani's favorable assumptions, these ratios are small compared with the ratio of aggregate saving to income, which is around 10 percent. The actual saving–income ratio was three to four times larger than the predictions of the life-cycle model. Nor is it surprising that a less than 1 percentage point change—as large as that may be relative to life-cycle saving—would be swamped by other determinants of aggregate saving.

A decrease in economic uncertainty might reduce the amount of assets held jointly for bequests and for precaution against emergencies. This would result in a decrease of intergenerational transfers relative to life-cycle saving. However, it is not clear how economic uncertainty varied over this period. These years included the Panic of 1907 and the Depression of 1920–1921. This possible explanation also appears tenuous at best.

While it is possible that special factors offset the rise in the saving–income ratio caused by increased retirement, life-cycle savings probably did not account for a large share of aggregate saving during this period. It appears that the difference between saving for retirement by workers and dissaving of retirement assets by retirees was small relative to the accumulation of assets for intergenerational transfers.

Life-Cycle Assets after Introduction of Social Security

The analysis in Chapter 2 showed that a person who expects to leave a bequest will hold a larger amount of assets at each age than an identical individual who plans no bequest and saves only to consume his life-cycle income more evenly over his life. Figure 7 combines the life-cycle asset patterns shown in Figures 2 and 3. The curve marked total assets is the life-cycle asset pattern of a person expecting to leave a bequest. The curve marked life-cycle assets shows the assets that an individual who did not expect to make a bequest would hold. The vertical distance between these two curves (plotted as bequest assets) is a measure of the assets held for bequest—and precautionary—purposes.

The largest possible reduction in saving resulting from the Feldstein-Munnell effect occurs if there is no induced change in retirement behavior. Under these conditions, social security taxes and benefits unambiguously reduce saving via income smoothing. Figure 8

FIGURE 7

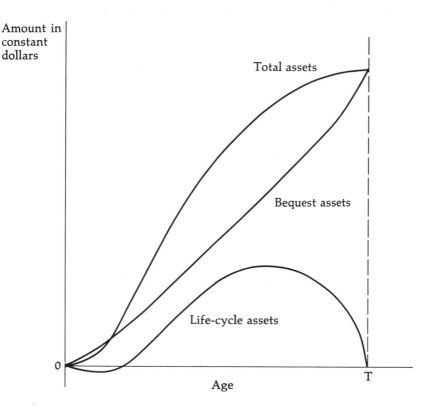

shows the effect of retiring at age sixty-five on the accumulation of assets, assuming no social security.[7] This will imply a kinked peak of life-cycle assets at retirement age because people would first accumulate funds for retirement at compound interest and then draw them down during the retirement years. During the accumulation period, interest adds more and more to total assets each year; during the retirement period, however, less interest is received and more must be taken from principal each year.[8]

[7] Age $R = 45$ (counting from an average entry into the labor force at age twenty).

[8] Drawing the figure for the expected age of death implies that the individual either buys a life annuity with life-cycle assets at time R or—because of the high loading cost of doing so—allows the actual value of the bequest to vary with length of life.

FIGURE 8

DIVISION OF TOTAL ASSETS WITH RETIREMENT BUT
WITHOUT SOCIAL SECURITY

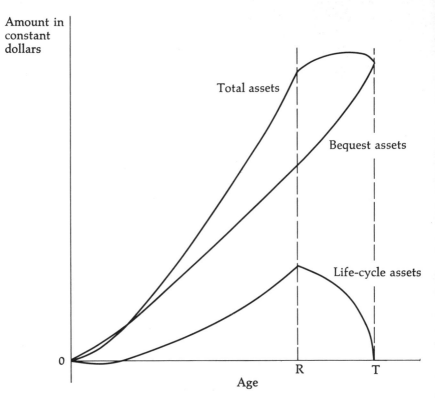

The Feldstein-Munnell effect of the introduction of social security is shown in Figure 9, assuming no changes in retirement and neglecting other effects discussed in Chapter 2. Life-cycle assets at retirement (age R) are reduced by the value of an annuity equivalent in value to the social security benefits. Before retirement, people reduce their saving each year by the amount of social security taxes. These taxes have an accumulated annuity value at age R equal (assuming actuarial fairness) to the value of the benefit stream. So the desired level of life-cycle assets is reduced everywhere except at the beginning and the end of life—where they are zero.

The reduction of assets depicted in Figure 9 is the maximum possible Feldstein-Munnell effect. Two alternative estimates of this maximum possible effect have been made: one using aggregate benefit data and another using detailed survey data on household assets.

FIGURE 9

FELDSTEIN-MUNNELL EFFECT OF SOCIAL SECURITY
ON ASSETS WITH NO INDUCED RETIREMENT

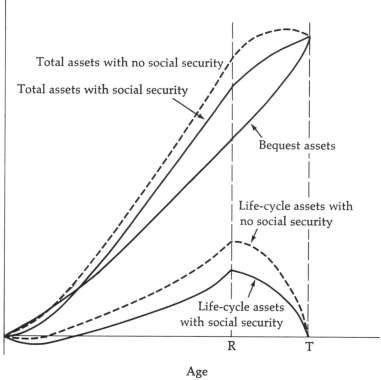

Both estimates compute the amount required at age sixty-five to pay the average social security benefits received over the remaining expected life of thirteen years. This amount is assumed to be built up between the ages of twenty and sixty-five and then drawn down over the retirement years. To estimate the maximum (dollar-for-dollar) effect on total assets, the life-cycle asset equivalent of social security for the group at age sixty-five is adjusted for the probability of living to sixty-five and for the larger life-cycle earnings of younger age groups.

Feldstein estimated that in 1971 the private capital stock was reduced by $2,029 billion (or 37 percent).[9] This estimate is net of the

9 Feldstein, "Social Security, Induced Retirement, and Aggregate Capital Ac-

increase in saving caused by induced retirement and thus ought to be well below the maximum possible Feldstein-Munnell effect, unless other effects were operative.

In 1971, total social security retirement benefits were $33.4 billion. Divided by the expected life at age sixty-five of 13.0 years, this amounts to an average of $2.57 billion for each age group.[10] This has an annuity value of $27.33, $22.75, or $19.24 billion, depending on whether it is assumed that the average real yield is 3, 6, or 9 percent a year, respectively. These alternative benchmarks were used to estimate the assets that otherwise would be accumulated by younger age groups and held by older age groups when allowance is made for the growth in life-cycle earnings and population and for mortality.[11] Details of the computations are given in the appendix to this chapter.

The total life-cycle assets that would otherwise be held by all age groups were estimated to be $943 billion at an interest rate of 3 percent, $612 billion at 6 percent, and $418 billion at 9 percent. A 3 percent real interest rate corresponds to—it is actually a bit under— the effective yield on social security and is identical to the rate used by Feldstein. The estimated maximum possible Feldstein-Munnell effect is a $943 billion reduction in the capital stock, less than half Feldstein's estimate. Higher interest rates approaching the 10 percent yield implicit in aggregate consumer behavior would imply an even lower maximum.[12] If these estimates are applied to the same wealth base that Feldstein used, the corresponding maximum percentage reductions in the capital stock are 21 percent, 15 percent, and 11 percent, depending on the interest rate.

In view of the large discrepancy between these estimates and those of Feldstein, cross-section data of asset holdings over the life-

cumulation," p. 922. This estimate was Feldstein's *gross* social security wealth estimate, which he noted "is remarkably close to the predicted long-run effect of 38 percent" based on his time series estimates of the consumption function. The problems with both estimates are discussed at length in Chapter 4 below.

[10] This average is biased upward by benefits received by retirees under sixty-five and downward by lower benefits received by retirees over sixty-five. There is little reason to suppose that the net bias is significant. The data for total benefits are from U.S. Social Security Administration, *Social Security Bulletin, Annual Statistical Supplement, 1973*, Table 28, p. 58. The data for life expectancy are for white males, aged sixty-five, in 1967, from U.S. Bureau of the Census, *Statistical Abstract of the United States: 1971* (92nd edition), Table 70, p. 53.

[11] It appears unnecessary to allow for any further growth in the coverage of the program since coverage of total paid employment was 79.5 percent in 1951, 85.3 percent in 1955, 87.9 percent in 1961, and 89.4 percent in 1971. See *Social Security Bulletin, Annual Statistical Supplement, 1973*, Table 27, p. 57.

[12] See Darby, "Consumer Expenditure Function."

cycle were also analyzed. The 1967 Survey of Economic Opportunity contains detailed data on assets, liabilities, and income for U.S. families.[13] The results reported here are primarily for white families.[14]

The data in the survey for total net worth approximate most closely the concept of total assets used in the previous theoretical discussion. This measure of total net worth includes nonhuman assets such as business, land, home, automobiles, bank accounts, stocks, and bonds, and is net of debts (both personal and those associated with the included assets). Some assets are omitted, however, such as household furnishings, most consumers' durable goods, clothing, rights to pension funds, and life insurance contracts.

Average total net worth by age of the head of household is plotted in Figure 10 over the period of working life and expected retirement.[15] Because of the large sampling variance, overlapping three-year moving averages are plotted. Total net worth rises rapidly during the working life and then flattens out around age sixty at about $30,000.[16] This pattern is consistent with a life-cycle model with retirement and substantial expected bequests.

The omission of the value of private and government pension rights from total net worth would underestimate both total and life-cycle assets by an equal amount. A correction was made based on the reported income stream of retirees from these sources.[17] The estimated life-cycle assets resulting from private and government pension funds also varies with the interest rate used in the calculations. Figure 11 shows the estimated net worth inclusive of pension funds for the lowest interest rate, 3 percent. This would give the largest estimate of life-cycle assets. Inclusion of pension rights results in a more definite peak with noticeable dissaving during the retirement years. Figure 11 is still quite consistent with the combined life-cycle and positive-bequest model.

---

[13] James P. Smith generously provided a clean data tape and advice on its use. Programming was done by Franklin Berger and computations were made by the RAND Corporation.

[14] The data for nonwhite families appeared insufficiently reliable for the current study, although checks were made to confirm that the basic conclusions were not dependent on their exclusion.

[15] The Survey of Economic Opportunity (SEO) oversampled poor households but provided weights for correcting the sample to correspond to the U.S. population. Those weights were used in computing the averages reported here.

[16] The dollar amounts are based on 1966 prices and wealth.

[17] The average income stream from these sources for families with a head aged sixty-five through seventy-seven was $387.23 a year. This implies a benchmark asset value at age sixty-five of $4,639.70 at 3 percent interest, $3,862.06 at 6 percent, and $3,266.14 at 9 percent.

FIGURE 10

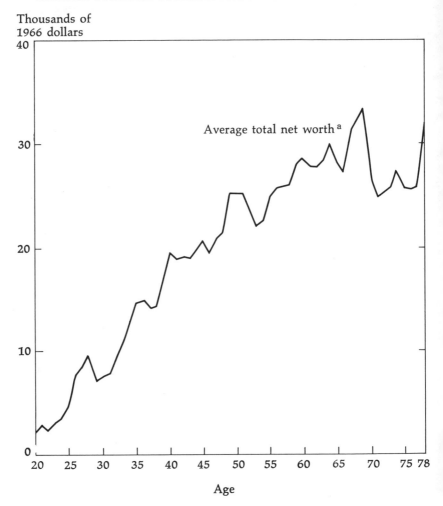

Thousands of
1966 dollars

a Survey of Economic Opportunity concept.

The next step was to divide these estimates of total assets into separate life-cycle and bequest portions. The life-cycle asset benchmark at age sixty-five was computed as the value of an annuity required to finance the estimated consumption stream derived from them.[18] Separate breakdowns were made for each of the three interest

[18] The details of the calculation are as follows. Consumption during the expected retirement period was estimated as income less the increase in assets; see

34

FIGURE 11

AVERAGE TOTAL NET WORTH INCLUSIVE OF IMPUTED PENSION RIGHTS BY AGE OF THE HEAD OF HOUSEHOLD, USING AN INTEREST RATE OF 3 PERCENT

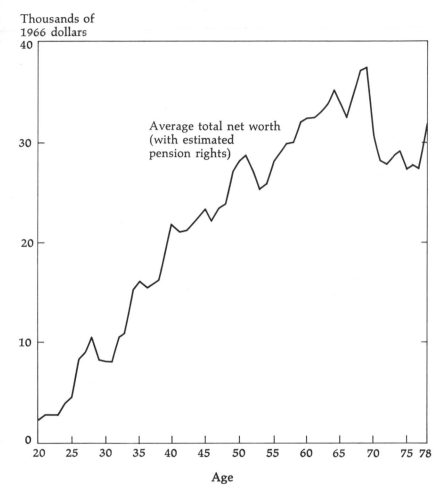

Thousands of
1966 dollars

Average total net worth
(with estimated
pension rights)

Age

James P. Smith, "Assets, Savings, and Labor Supply," *Economic Inquiry*, vol. 15 (October 1977), pp. 551-73. This consumption stream was reduced by current nonasset income (labor earnings, unemployment compensation, public welfare, and the like) and social security benefits. When this reduced consumption stream is averaged, it yields the average consumption stream to be financed by life-cycle assets. Since age sixty-five retirees would have higher life-cycle earnings, these averages were adjusted upward by the normal growth in per capita income for six and a half years (half of expected retirement): $(1.0185)^{6.5} = 1.1266$. This estimated consumption stream was then converted into an annuity value at 3, 6, rates previously used. Figure 12 shows the life-cycle and bequest portions of total assets using an interest rate of 3 percent. Smaller estimates of life-cycle assets would correspond to higher interest rates.

The estimated amount of per capital life-cycle and bequest assets by age can be used to compute the aggregate amount of assets implied by steady-state growth, taking account of the growth in the number of persons in each age group and of mortality.[19] It is estimated that life-cycle assets account for 28.5, 18.9, and 13.0 percent of total assets for 3, 6, and 9 percent interest rates, respectively. These estimates err, if anything, on the high side. This evidence suggests that the potential effects of social security on bequest assets may be important. The Feldstein estimate does not seem consistent with his life-cycle approach.

Another estimate of the maximum possible Feldstein-Munnell effect was made by obtaining a life-cycle asset benchmark at age sixty-five inclusive of the annuity value of social security benefits and assuming that the difference in life-cycle assets represents a dollar-for-dollar reduction in total assets.[20] The age sixty-five benchmark values for social security wealth were $15,125, $12,590, and $10,647 for 3, 6, and 9 percent interest rates, respectively. The fraction of total assets inclusive of the imputed value of pensions and social security represented by social security wealth was estimated as 23.1, 16.7, or 12.1 percent, depending on the interest rate.

The cross-section estimates of the maximum possible Feldstein-Munnell effect are similar to the estimated maximum effect of 21, 15, and 11 percent derived earlier from aggregate benefit data for 1971. If Feldstein had used his estimate of net social security wealth—a more appropriate concept than gross social security wealth in terms of the life-cycle model—for calculating the dollar-for-dollar replacement of the capital stock, his estimate of the reduction in the capital stock would have been 25 percent instead of 37 percent. These three

---

and 9 percent interest to derive three alternative benchmark estimates of life-cycle assets at age sixty-five. Life-cycle assets for other ages were then computed as described in the appendix to this chapter.

Smith suggested an alternative consumption concept that added to the cash consumption concept an imputed yield of 5 percent on owned assets. This concept was also tried, but no substantial differences arose when account was taken of the imputed yield in selecting interest rates for computing asset values. (The total implicit yield is then the 5 percent imputed service yield plus the 2 to 3 percent reported pecuniary yield.)

[19] That is, each successive age group was assumed to be 1.4 percent larger than the next previous group at age twenty. The weighting of older ages was also reduced by the probability of death since age twenty.

[20] The same procedure that was applied to private and government pensions was used for social security.

FIGURE 12

DIVISION OF AVERAGE TOTAL NET WORTH INCLUSIVE OF IMPUTED PENSION
RIGHTS BETWEEN ASSETS HELD FOR LIFE-CYCLE CONSUMPTION SMOOTHING
AND ASSETS HELD IN EXPECTATION OF BEQUESTS, USING AN
INTEREST RATE OF 3 PERCENT

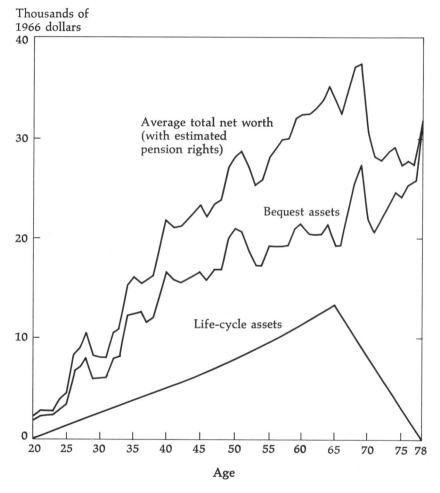

Thousands of
1966 dollars

Average total net worth
(with estimated
pension rights)

Bequest assets

Life-cycle assets

Age

different approaches estimate that the net social security wealth is
21 to 25 percent of the sum of the capital stock and net social security
wealth using an interest rate of 3 percent. These estimates would be
nearly halved if the 9 percent interest rate were used.

It should be emphasized that these are upper limits for the
Feldstein-Munnell effect. If social security induces persons to retire at

an earlier age, this would reduce the effect on the capital stock below the estimated maximum amount. Other factors may also affect the impact of social security on the saving–income ratio. To the extent that social security benefits replace support from children or welfare during retirement, there is no change in the life cycle of income or in saving.[21] In addition, both the possible wealth loss and the uncertainty of social security would tend to increase saving. On the other hand, the forced annuity purchase may reduce the precautionary value of expected bequests. Although Feldstein's estimates appear to be too high, the importance of bequests in total wealth and saving could conceivably result in a reduction in the capital stock larger than the value of net social security wealth.

Appendix: Estimating Life-Cycle Assets from Retirement Age Benchmarks

In order to estimate the assets now held for life-cycle purposes at different ages if people aged sixty-five hold an amount L_{65}, it is necessary to take account of growth in population and life-cycle earnings and of mortality.

If growth is steady, the real amount of assets held by people then aged sixty-five will grow each year at the same rate as real income, say g. The amount held per capita will grow at this rate less the growth rate (say π) of population, or $g - \pi$. Looking at aggregate data, people should be viewed at age a as accumulating toward or decumulating from an amount equal to the benchmark amount adjusted for compounded growth—that is, $(1 + g)^{65-a} \cdot L_{65}$. For per capita data (such as the Survey of Economic Opportunity), the corresponding amount is $(1 + g - \pi)^{65-a} \cdot L_{65}$.

For per capita data, it is necessary to allow for the fact that mortality reduces the cost at younger ages of an annuity that starts paying at age sixty-five. In other words, the expected value of life-cycle assets at age sixty-five is less than the value of assets held by those who actually live to age sixty-five. The probability that one is alive at sixty-five if he is alive at age a is denoted by P_{65}^a. Then the expected life-cycle assets at age sixty-five of people now age a is $P_{65}^a \cdot (1 + g - \pi)^{65-a} \cdot L_{65}$. For aggregate data by age group, no such adjustment is required since the assets are to be accumulated by the age group as a whole.

---

[21] Alicia H. Munnell, *The Future of Social Security* (Washington, D.C.: Brookings Institution, 1977), p. 123, summarizes various surveys of OASDHI beneficiaries which indicate a significant decline from the 1940s to the 1960s in the percentage receiving public assistance and contributions from relatives.

Because of the life-cycle growth in earnings, one would expect life-cycle saving from labor earnings to be concentrated in middle age. This would imply less life-cycle assets at each age than if the amount saved were the amount required to accumulate expected assets at age sixty-five over forty-five years of equal payments accumulated at interest. This latter amount is therefore a safe upper estimate of life-cycle assets. For per capita data, life-cycle assets at age a $(20 \leq a < 65)$ is estimated as:

$$L_a = s(a - 20, r) \cdot \frac{P_{65}^{a} \cdot (1 + g - \pi)^{65-a} \cdot L_{65}}{s(45, r)}, \tag{1}$$

where $s(x, r)$ is the amount accumulated by saving \$1 a year for x years at an annually compounded interest rate r.[22] The ratio gives the number of dollars that would have to be saved annually to accumulate the expected life-cycle assets at age sixty-five over a working life of forty-five years. This is multiplied by $s(a - 20, r)$ to obtain the amount that would be accumulated by saving at that rate since age twenty. The corresponding formula for aggregate data by age group is:[23]

$$L_a = s(a - 20, r) \cdot \frac{(1 + g)^{65-a} \cdot L_{65}}{s(45, r)}. \tag{2}$$

The value of life-cycle assets for ages over sixty-five can be approximated by assuming that everyone who reaches age sixty-five lives his expected life of thirteen years and then dies. This avoids getting into the very old ages for which data on total assets are unreliable. Thus, life-cycle assets are assumed to be drawn down by a constant consumption stream until they are exhausted at the end of thirteen years. Until then, the remaining balance earns interest at the annually compounded rate r. For per capita data, life-cycle assets at age a $(65 < a < 78)$ is estimated as:

$$L_a = v(78 - a, r) \frac{(1 + g - \pi)^{65-a} \cdot L_{65}}{v(13, r)}, \tag{3}$$

---

[22] A well-known actuarial formula gives $s(x, r) = [(1 + r)^x - 1]/r$. For computational purposes equation (1) can be simplified to:

$$L_a = \frac{(1 + r)^{a-20} - 1}{(1 + r)^{45} - 1} \cdot P_{65}^{a} \cdot (1 + g - \pi)^{65-a} \cdot L_{65}. \tag{1'}$$

[23] For computations, this is:

$$L_a = \frac{(1 + r)^{a-20} - 1}{(1 + r)^{45} - 1} \cdot (1 + g)^{65-a} \cdot L_{65}. \tag{2'}$$

where $v(x, r)$ is the present value of $1 a year for x years at an annually compounded interest rate r.[24] The ratio gives the number of dollars per year for thirteen years that could have been bought with age sixty-five assets, and $v(78 - a, r)$ gives the values of that stream of dollars per year for the remaining years of life. The corresponding formula for aggregate data by age group:[25]

$$L_a = v(78 - a, r) \frac{(1 + g)^{65-a} \cdot L_{65}}{v(13, r)}. \tag{4}$$

These formulas are used to derive estimates of life-cycle assets for alternative interest rates and values of life-cycle assets at age sixty-five. The estimates are probably high. In each case, real income growth and population growth were estimated by their long-run average values of 3.25 and 1.4 percent a year, respectively.[26]

---

[24] A well-known actuarial formula gives $v(x, r) = [1 - (1 + r)^{-x}]/r$. For computations, this formula was used:

$$L_a = \frac{1 - (1 + r)^{a-78}}{1 - (1 + r)^{-13}} \cdot (1 + g - \pi)^{65-a} \cdot L_{65}. \tag{3'}$$

[25] For computations, this is:

$$L_a = \frac{1 - (1 + r)^{a-76}}{1 - (1 + r)^{-13}} \cdot (1 + g)^{65-a} \cdot L_{65}. \tag{4'}$$

[26] See U.S. Bureau of Economic Analysis, *Long-Term Economic Growth 1860–1970* (1973), pp. 105, 107.

4

Direct Estimates of the Effect of Social Security on the Saving–Income Ratio

The question of whether and by how much social security reduces (or increases) the ratio of private saving to private income is strictly empirical. Previous work has involved two major approaches: (1) international comparisons of saving–income ratios with the scale of social security programs, and other variables; (2) estimation of consumption (or saving) functions using the U.S. aggregate time series data. Neither approach has yielded consistent answers.

Although significant reductions in the saving–income ratio have been found in some international comparisons, in other studies the effect of social security is not statistically distinguishable from zero. In all these studies, the issue of reverse causality has arisen because the level of saving in a country may affect the demand for a social security program.

The time series regressions have also been inconclusive. Feldstein estimated a 38 percent reduction in the private saving–income ratio. However, after correction of his calculations, his results imply a reduction of only 26 percent. Munnell estimated a reduction of only 5 percent, whereas Barro obtained no evidence of any reduction. The Feldstein and Barro results depend on the respective sides they take on a methodological issue.

New estimates for several alternative measures of the scale of the social security program are reported in this chapter. A reduction of 25 to 30 percent in the private saving–income ratio is estimated using data for 1929–1940 and 1947–1974. This reduction is significant on economic grounds, but it does not differ from zero at conventional levels of statistical significance. If the estimation is confined to the postwar period, there is no evidence of an economically or statistically significant reduction in this ratio. The estimates made by both Feldstein and this study using 1930s data probably contain an upward bias and may serve as an upper limit to the possible reduction in the saving–income ratio. The results are consistent with the estimate of the largest possible Feldstein-Munnell effect in Chapter 3.

Previous Direct Estimates

Few empirical studies of the magnitude of the social security program's effects on saving have been performed. This is surprising in view of the size of the program.

International Comparisons. International comparisons have been made by Henry Aaron and Martin Feldstein. In his original analysis using 1957 data, Aaron related the household saving–disposable income ratio for twenty-two countries to income, to the social security expenditures–national income ratio, and to other variables.[1] A significant negative effect of the social security expenditures–national income ratio was found. Although this would appear to imply that social security reduced private saving, Aaron also considered the inverse hypothesis that countries with low saving would tend to have high social security expenditures because of greater "need." No attempt was made to disentangle the direction of causality or the relative size of these influences. In a later study using 1960 data which Aaron wrote with Joseph Pechman and Michael Taussig, the negative correlation between the social security expenditures–national income ratio and the saving–income ratio was statistically not significantly different from zero.[2]

Feldstein's estimates are based on a sample of fifteen countries using data averaged over the late 1950s.[3] So many different variables and equation forms were tried on a limited data base that his results are not very convincing. Feldstein did obtain "significantly" negative partial correlations between certain measures of the scale of a social security program and the private saving–income ratio. Although he used an elaborate life-cycle model in which the expected retirement–expected life ratio affects saving and is also affected by the social

---

[1] Henry Aaron, "Social Security: International Comparisons," in *Studies in the Economics of Income Maintenance*, ed. Otto Eckstein (Washington, D.C.: Brookings Institution, 1967).

[2] Joseph A. Pechman, Henry J. Aaron, and Michael K. Taussig, "Appendix D: International Comparisons," in *Social Security: Perspectives for Reform* (Washington, D.C.: Brookings Institution, 1968).

[3] Martin Feldstein, "Social Security and Private Savings: International Evidence in an Extended Life Cycle Model," Harvard Institute of Economic Research, Discussion Paper Number 361 (May 1974).

security program, no attempt was made to deal with the problems of reverse causality. The international comparisons appear to be plagued with serious questions of the direction of causality and with data of limited quality and quantity.

Time Series Analyses. The two major time series studies published to date are by Alicia H. Munnell and Martin Feldstein.[4] These studies are closely related.[5] They utilize an extended version of the Ando-Modigliani life-cycle model in which social security has offsetting effects on saving: a decrease because of a smoothing of life-cycle earnings and an increase because of an induced increase in the ratio of expected retirement to expected working life.

Munnell's results. Munnell's empirical work is summarized in an article in the *National Tax Journal.*[6] For personal saving (disposable personal income — personal outlays), she found *no* statistically significant effects from either the income-smoothing variable (social security contributions ≈ benefits) or the retirement variable (labor force participation of males sixty-five and older). Her results were essentially the same when an estimate of social security wealth was used as the income-smoothing variable. The coefficient estimates combined with the estimate of induced retirement indicate a rather small net negative impact of social security on saving.[7] However, no change in saving for given income and other variables does not mean no change in saving if the induced retirement reduces income; this is the subject of Chapter 5. Munnell examined a retirement-saving concept measuring the change in certain assets (life insurance company assets less policy loans, pension plans, and government insurance and pension plans) for which she obtained some statistically significant results.[8] Combined with the estimated effects on personal saving,

---

[4] Alicia H. Munnell, *The Effect of Social Security on Personal Saving* (Cambridge, Mass.: Ballinger Publishing Co., 1974); Martin Feldstein, "Social Security, Induced Retirement, and Aggregate Capital Accumulation," *Journal of Political Economy*, vol. 82 (September/October 1974), pp. 905–26.

[5] Feldstein was a member of Munnell's thesis committee and Munnell assisted Feldstein in calculating his social security wealth variable. Indeed, they are in turn related to the earlier Brookings Institution work in view of Pechman, Aaron, and Taussig's acknowledgment in their *Perspectives for Reform* (p. viii) of "a major debt of gratitude to Alicia Munnell whose role far exceeded that of a research assistant."

[6] Alicia H. Munnell, "The Impact of Social Security on Personal Savings," *National Tax Journal*, vol. 27 (December 1974), pp. 553–67.

[7] This is for the 1900–1971 and the 1929–1971 regressions. A larger effect is estimated for the 1946–1971 regressions, but Munnell rightly points out that these inconsistent results are probably because of omitted variables.

[8] Munnell, "Impact of Social Security on Personal Savings," p. 557.

this would suggest that social security has affected the type of financial investments held, but not aggregate saving and capital formation.

Feldstein's results. Martin Feldstein's widely discussed 1974 article is the principal evidence that the social security program has had a large effect on the saving–income ratio.[9] His empirical work is based on a 1963 Ando-Modigliani consumption function.[10] The complete mathematical specification of the consumption function used by Feldstein is:

$$C_t = \alpha + \beta_1 Y_t + \beta_2 RE_t + \beta_3 Y_{t-1} + \beta_4 U_t + \gamma_1 W_{t-1} + \gamma_2 SSW_t, \tag{5}$$

where C_t = consumer expenditures [11]

$\quad Y_t$ = disposable personal income

$\quad RE_t$ = gross undistributed corporate profits

$\quad U_t$ = unemployment rate

$\quad W_t$ = wealth at the end of the year [12]

$\quad SSW_t$ = present value of social security benefits, measured either gross ($SSWG_t$) or net ($SSWN_t$) of future taxes on those in the labor force.

This consumption function is only one of many alternatives that could have been chosen.[13] Although this consumption function might have characteristics that biased the results, there is no particular reason to suppose that this is the case.

Consumer expenditures appear to be explained by four principal factors: permanent income or the normal income stream from total human and nonhuman wealth, transitory income or the difference between current and permanent income, excess money supply, and the stock of consumers' durable goods. Although the excess money supply is omitted from Feldstein's consumption function, it should be uncorrelated with social security wealth (SSW) so that no bias in the estimated γ_2 is introduced.[14] Also, there is no obvious reason why the omission of the stock of consumers' durables would introduce a

---

[9] Feldstein, "Social Security, Induced Retirement, and Aggregate Capital Accumulation."

[10] Albert Ando and Franco Modigliani, "The Life Cycle Hypothesis of Saving: Aggregate Implications and Tests," *American Economic Review*, vol. 53 (March 1963), pp. 55–84.

[11] All variables except U_t were measured in 1958 dollars per capita.

[12] Feldstein used Ando and Modigliani's estimates of per capita household net worth as used in the FRB-MIT model.

[13] Several of these alternatives are discussed below.

[14] Bias is introduced only when the omitted variables are correlated with included variables.

bias in γ_2, although the low level of the stock in 1947 after World War II and the big jump in social security wealth in that year might create problems.[15]

Permanent income and transitory income are probably captured by the variables Y_t, RE_t, Y_{t-1}, U_t, and W_{t-1}. Disposable personal income plus (net) undistributed corporate profits is nearly the entire income available to the private sector for consumption or saving.[16] Taken together, these five variables serve to estimate the levels and coefficients of permanent and transitory income—say, $\delta_1 Y_{Pt} + \delta_2 Y_{Tt}$. Social security wealth might serve as a proxy for human wealth, but the unemployment rate also captures differences of current labor income from what would normally be expected. Although there might be some positive bias in the estimated γ_2, it is probably small.

Feldstein's social security wealth data are based on estimates made by Munnell.[17] Munnell estimated gross social security wealth (SSWG) as real personal disposable income per capita times a constant benefit ratio (0.41) times a weighted sum of numbers of persons covered by social security. The weighted sum is for various age, sex, and marital groups, with the weights reflecting projected future benefit streams with changes anticipated in widows' benefits assumed. Feldstein's measure of gross social security wealth changes because of (1) changes in real disposable per capita income, (2) the numbers covered and their age-sex-marital distribution, and (3) changes in the benefit formula for widows.[18] Since real disposable income per capita is already included in the equation, SSWG per capita will capture only interactions of this variable with the weighted-and-benefit-adjusted coverage per capita.

Feldstein obtained a "statistically significant" SSW coefficient for four alternative estimates of social security wealth for the sample that included the prewar years 1929–1940. In no case was SSW statistically significant when the regressions were estimated only for the years

---

[15] Feldstein excluded the war years 1941–1946 so that changes over this period first appear in the 1947 data. The stock of consumers' durable goods will be considered further below.

[16] Feldstein uses gross undistributed corporate profits (inclusive of capital consumption allowances) but notes that it does not significantly alter the results if he uses the net concept.

[17] See Munnell, *The Effect of Social Security on Personal Saving*, pp. 121–26, for details. Feldstein's preferred gross social security wealth (SSWG1) concept, for example, is Munnell's series SSW for discount rate $= 3$ and growth rate $= 2$ multiplied by the ratio of the price index in 1971 to the price index in 1958 (that is, approximately 1.343) to convert her figures to 1971 dollars.

[18] Net social security wealth also varies because of pre-1971 variations in the ratio of taxes to disposable income since this ratio is assumed to be anticipated correctly before 1971 and to be constant after 1970.

1947–1971. However, Feldstein did not include the unemployment rate in the regressions for which significant SSW coefficients were estimated. When Feldstein estimated his full specification—equation (5)—the coefficient of SSWG was positive but not statistically distinguishable from zero.[19] Therefore, his conclusion that social security increased consumption and decreased saving depends critically upon (1) deleting the unemployment rate from the equation and (2) including the prewar data.

Feldstein's argument for excluding the unemployment rate variable presumes that SSW should be included and the unemployment rate excluded unless proven otherwise.[20] This is precisely the reverse of standard statistical practice and scientific method. Normally, a newly proposed variable, particularly one of ambiguous sign, must prove its ability to add to the existing model. On this basis, an effect of social security wealth is rejected because, for the 1929–1971 regression reported, the unemployment rate is significant just at the 0.10 level on the appropriate one-tailed t-test while the SSW coefficient fails the appropriate two-tailed test even at the 0.20 level.[21] Feldstein argues that the insignificance of the 1947–1971 SSW coefficients (even with U_t deleted) should be forgiven because they are similar in magnitude to those estimated for 1929–1971. This too seems questionable. Since a positive bias was to be anticipated in the estimated coefficient of SSW to the extent that SSW serves as a partial proxy for human wealth, it is not surprising that there is a "significant" positive coefficient when the unemployment rate is deleted. Although Feldstein's study indicates that social security might have some effect on saving and consumption, his results are not very convincing.

Feldstein's estimate of the effect of social security on saving is not fully supported by his published results. Even if methodological objections are set aside and the analysis is restricted to the 1929–1971 regressions which delete U_t, a smaller estimate would seem appropriate. First, Feldstein used the coefficient of gross social security

---

[19] Reference is made here to Feldstein, "Social Security, Induced Retirement, and Aggregate Capital Accumulation," p. 917, equations 2.6 and 2.10. Only results for the SSWG1 concept were reported.

[20] Ibid., p. 919.

[21] Feldstein argues that the statistical problems with the SSW coefficient are not because of (partial) multicollinearity with the unemployment rate. His grounds appear to be entirely spurious. For the 1929–1971 regression inclusive of both SSW_t and U_t, the coefficients of W_{t-1} and SSW_t are practically identical (0.013 and 0.010, respectively). When Feldstein constrains them to be equal (0.012) and finds only a marginal improvement in the significance of the U_t coefficient (to the 0.08 level), he is nearly rerunning the original regression with the significance of the constrained coefficient because of the W_{t-1} dog and not the SSW_t tail.

wealth, 0.021, instead of the larger 0.031 coefficient of net social security wealth. Applying 0.021 to the larger SSWG1 amount results in an estimated saving reduction of $43 billion instead of $37 billion for SSWN1. But SSWN1 both fits better statistically and is preferable to SSWG1 in terms of the life-cycle model. Second, Feldstein added to this $43 billion another $18 billion for the effect of the reduction in disposable income because of social security taxes. But disposable income is increased by an equal amount by social security benefits so that there is no net effect on disposable income or saving. Correcting for these two factors would yield an estimated reduction of $37 billion instead of $61 billion in 1971, or a 26 percent reduction in private saving as opposed to a 38 percent reduction.

In Chapter 3, the maximum possible reduction in the capital stock resulting from the Feldstein-Munnell effect was estimated to be approximately 21 percent using aggregate benefit data. In that chapter, it was estimated that the value of the life-cycle asset equivalent of social security using a 3 percent interest rate was $943 billion. This is quite close to Feldstein's 1971 SSWN1 value of $1,162 billion.[22] But the total Feldstein-Munnell effect allowing for induced retirement should be less than the value of net social security wealth. Either this smaller 26 percent effect is too high or social security has other—presumably bequest—effects on private saving.

Barro's results. Barro's time series analysis of the effects of social security overlaps with the current study.[23] He starts with the same consumer expenditure function used below. However, his proxies for permanent and transitory income are similar to Feldstein's and include an unemployment variable. In Barro's results, the unemployment variable is always significant, whereas social security (using either Feldstein's or Barro's concept) is not except when the unemployment term is deleted. The estimated social security coefficient is both positive and negative, depending on the particular definitions used for the variables and the period over which the equations are estimated. Barro's study supports the view that there is a lack of evidence that social security has any effect on saving.

---

[22] If Feldstein had calculated the effect assuming that the $1,162 billion would otherwise have been held as capital stock, he would have gotten 25 percent as opposed to 37 percent using SSWG1.

[23] See Robert J. Barro, *The Impact of Social Security on Private Saving: Evidence from the U.S. Time Series* (Washington, D.C.: American Enterprise Institute, 1978).

New Direct Time Series Estimates

The permanent income approach has been widely used as a method of estimating the normal yield from human and nonhuman wealth (that is, permanent income) and comparing that yield with current income. This approach is more congenial to analysis of saving for bequests than is the life-cycle approach, but this is more a matter of analytical convenience than any real difference. In the following analysis, a social security variable will be added to a permanent income consumption function.

The Expanded Consumer Expenditure Function. The following analysis uses the consumer expenditure function developed in another study.[24] This approach combines in one equation factors affecting pure consumption and net investment in consumers' durable goods. This combined function has good explanatory power—the ratio of the standard error to the mean for annual data from 1947 to 1973 is 5.0 percent for private saving and 0.6 percent for consumer expenditures.[25] Because there is less "background noise" in the estimates, it may be possible to get a more precise estimate of the effect of social security.

The mathematical specification of this consumer expenditure function is:

$$
(6)
$$
$$
C_t = \beta_0 + \beta_1 Y_{Pt} + \beta_2 Y_{Tt} + \beta_3 M_t + \beta_4 D_{t-1} + \beta_5 (P_D/P_{ND})_t + \beta_6 i_t,
$$

where
C_t = consumer expenditures
Y_{Pt} = permanent income
Y_{Tt} = transitory income
M_t = real money balances
D_t = the stock of consumers' durable goods at the end of the year
$(P_D/P_{ND})_t$ = the ratio of the prices of durable and nondurable goods
i_t = the market interest rate.

The analysis in Chapter 2 suggests that, given the level of income, the social security program can affect consumption (and

---

[24] Michael R. Darby, "The Consumer Expenditure Function," *Explorations in Economic Research*, vol. 4 (Winter/Spring 1977–1978), pp. 645–74. For a convenient summary, see also Darby, "Postwar U.S. Consumption, Consumer Expenditures and Saving," *American Economic Review, Papers and Proceedings*, vol. 65 (May 1975), pp. 217–22.

[25] This latter number corresponds to an R^2 (adjusted) of 0.9996 and a Durbin-Watson statistic of 2.37.

hence consumer expenditures) through (1) the Feldstein-Munnell effect, (2) the negative wealth effect that results if the real interest rate is higher than the implicit yield on social security, (3) a negative uncertainty-of-receipt effect, and (4) a positive-bequest effect resulting from the fact that people are required to belong to the social security system. If the second and third effects are small, the overall effect of social security on consumption would probably be a larger increase than would be predicted by the Feldstein-Munnell effect alone.

To analyze the total effect of social security on saving, a term $\beta_7 SS_t$ is added to equation (6). If the estimated β_7 is significantly positive, this would imply that the net effect of social security is to reduce saving, other things being equal, and vice versa if β_7 is negative. Four alternative measures of the scale of social security were used: the Feldstein-Munnell net and gross social security wealth concepts (SSWN1 and SSWG1), Barro's benefit x coverage variable,[26] and OASI taxes paid (SSTax).[27]

Empirical Estimates. The expanded consumer expenditure function was estimated for data from 1929 through 1974 exclusive of the war years 1941–1946. These were the first and last years for which reasonably consistent data series were available for all the variables. All variables except $(P_D/P_{ND})_t$ and i_t are measured in billions of 1958 dollars. Sources are given in the appendix to this chapter. Both the M_1 and the M_2 concepts of money were used in the regressions (M_1 is currency and demand deposits; M_2 is M_1 plus bank time deposits). The narrow M_1 concept has performed better in postwar consumer expenditure functions than the broader M_2 concept. However, because the classification of demand deposits was largely arbitrary before the prohibition of interest payments on demand deposits in the Banking Acts of 1933 and 1935, the M_2 concept is used as an imperfect but consistent proxy for the medium of exchange.[28]

The estimates of the extended consumer expenditure function using Feldstein's SSWG1 and SSWN1 concepts are presented in Table 4 and those using Barro's benefit x coverage variable and social security taxes are presented in Table 5. As was expected, the M_2

---

[26] This is the product of (1) benefits per recipient in the old-age survivors and disability program, (2) the ratio of the number of workers with earnings taxable by social security at some time during the year to the total labor force, and (3) the total population. For details, see Barro, *The Impact of Social Security on Private Saving.*

[27] This variable treats (perhaps a fraction of) social security taxes as if they were viewed as income and savings.

[28] See Milton Friedman and Anna J. Schwartz, *A Monetary History of the United States, 1867–1960* (Princeton, N.J.: Princeton University Press, 1963).

TABLE 4

Extended Consumer Expenditure Function Estimates Based on Feldstein's Social Security Wealth Variables

Reg. No.	SS_t Concept	M_t Concept	Period of Estimation[a]	Const.	Y_{Pt}	Y_{Tt}	M_t	D_{t-1}	$(P_D/P_{ND})_t$	i_t	SS_t	$\bar{R}^2$	SEE[c]	D-W[d]
									Estimated Coefficient of[b]					
1	SSWN1	M_2	1929–1974	21.65 (1.25)	0.835 (23.30)	0.546 (13.77)	0.039 (0.79)	−0.148 (−2.57)	−22.01 (−1.23)	3.54 (2.89)	0.025 (1.33)	0.9997	2.58	2.27
2	SSWN1	M_2	1947–1974	−5.36 (−0.09)	0.905 (13.36)	0.539 (6.90)	0.010 (1.15)	−0.178 (−2.25)	−14.56 (−0.32)	1.83 (0.90)	0.003 (0.09)	0.9995	2.97	2.33
3	SSWG1	M_2	1929–1974	26.34 (1.63)	0.821 (22.60)	0.541 (13.37)	0.042 (0.86)	−0.149 (−2.56)	−24.97 (−1.50)	3.60 (2.95)	0.017 (1.31)	0.9997	2.58	2.27
4	SSWG1	M_2	1947–1974	−0.19 (−0.00)	0.893 (12.66)	0.513 (5.63)	0.074 (0.89)	−0.203 (−2.27)	−13.13 (−0.29)	1.42 (0.65)	0.015 (0.50)	0.9995	2.95	2.29
5	SSWN1	M_1	1929–1974	21.54 (1.02)	0.841 (18.25)	0.553 (14.12)	0.164 (0.27)	−0.155 (−2.62)	−19.79 (−0.92)	3.48 (2.41)	0.033 (2.20)	0.9997	2.61	2.27
6	SSWN1	M_1	1947–1974	−139.11 (−2.49)	1.002 (17.92)	0.455 (7.42)	0.726 (4.31)	−0.229 (−3.97)	17.26 (0.50)	1.78 (1.19)	−0.017 (−0.79)	0.9997	2.21	2.40
7	SSWG1	M_1	1929–1974	25.44 (1.23)	0.830 (17.65)	0.549 (13.67)	0.005 (0.09)	−0.159 (−2.63)	−20.93 (−0.98)	3.38 (2.33)	0.024 (2.13)	0.9997	2.61	2.28
8	SSWG1	M_1	1947–1974	−137.64 (−2.40)	1.002 (16.76)	0.460 (6.77)	0.711 (4.08)	−0.226 (−3.58)	17.99 (0.51)	1.90 (1.20)	−0.011 (−0.59)	0.9997	2.22	2.42

[a] 1929–1974 regressions exclude the war years 1941–1946.

[b] The parentheses below the coefficient estimates give t-statistics. For explanations of the symbols, see equation (6).

[c] SEE is the standard error of estimate in billions of 1958 dollars.

[d] D-W is the Durbin-Watson statistic, adjusted for 1 gap for the 1929–1974 regressions.

TABLE 5

Extended Consumer Expenditure Function Estimates Based on Barro's Benefit-Coverage Variable and on OASI Taxes Paid

Reg. No.	SS_t Concept	M_t Concept	Period of Estimation[a]	Estimated Coefficient of[b]								$\bar{R}^2$	SEE[c]	D-W[d]
				Const.	Y_{Pt}	Y_{Tt}	M_t	D_{t-1}	$(P_D/P_{ND})_t$	i_t	SS_t			
9	Barro	M_2	1929–1974	32.09 (1.96)	0.822 (16.58)	0.553 (13.60)	0.087 (1.75)	−0.118 (−2.06)	−36.76 (−2.49)	3.97 (2.61)	0.011 (0.24)	0.9997	2.65	2.23
10	Barro	M_2	1947–1974	−6.37 (−0.11)	0.896 (11.91)	0.539 (7.47)	0.119 (1.65)	−0.185 (−2.30)	−14.90 (−0.33)	2.03 (0.98)	0.018 (0.26)	0.9995	2.97	2.37
11	SSTax	M_2	1929–1974	14.61 (0.75)	0.828 (23.31)	0.548 (13.97)	0.063 (1.55)	−0.147 (−2.61)	−15.48 (−0.76)	3.41 (2.76)	0.803 (1.42)	0.9997	2.57	2.26
12	SSTax	M_2	1947–1974	−8.05 (−0.13)	0.903 (13.36)	0.542 (7.58)	0.101 (1.72)	−0.178 (−2.47)	−11.71 (−0.24)	1.87 (0.95)	0.152 (0.19)	0.9995	2.97	2.32
13	Barro	M_1	1929–1974	34.65 (1.61)	0.870 (16.00)	0.585 (15.34)	0.028 (0.43)	−0.085 (−1.47)	−39.01 (−1.91)	3.03 (1.77)	−0.033 (−0.81)	0.9997	2.77	2.13
14	Barro	M_1	1947–1974	−126.67 (−2.34)	0.980 (18.17)	0.440 (7.45)	0.662 (4.46)	−0.250 (−4.16)	18.14 (0.51)	1.68 (1.09)	0.011 (0.28)	0.9997	2.24	2.42
15	SSTax	M_1	1929–1974	18.42 (0.82)	0.828 (17.30)	0.564 (14.81)	0.052 (0.87)	−0.143 (−2.45)	−16.68 (−0.72)	3.53 (2.41)	1.107 (1.98)	0.9997	2.64	2.23
16	SSTax	M_1	1947–1974	−126.16 (−2.33)	0.981 (18.00)	0.439 (7.40)	0.641 (4.49)	−0.246 (−4.30)	20.43 (0.55)	1.57 (1.05)	0.096 (0.17)	0.9997	2.24	2.41

a1929–1947 regressions exclude the war years 1941–1946.

bThe parentheses below the coefficient estimates give t-statistics. For explanations of the symbols, see equation (6).

cSEE is the standard error of estimate in billions of 1958 dollars.

dD-W is the Durbin-Watson statistic, adjusted for 1 gap for the 1929–1974 regressions.

definition of money does not do nearly so well as M_1 in the postwar regressions (the even-numbered regressions in Table 4 and 5). M_1 does even worse if it is used for the whole period 1929–1974 because of the inconsistency in economic meaning of the data for M_1 in the early part of the period. Because of the difficulty with the monetary data, this analysis of the results will emphasize the M_2 regressions for the 1929–1974 period and the M_1 regressions for the 1947–1974 period. The coefficients of the variables other than the social security variables, SS_t, present no surprises and will not be reviewed here.

In regressions 9, 10, 13, and 14, Barro's benefit x coverage variable was not significantly different from zero in either a statistical or an economic sense. Since no strong theoretical case was presented by Barro for using this variable, only small weight can be put on these results, showing essentially no effect of social security on private saving.

The other three social security scale variables—Feldstein's net and gross social security wealth (SSWN1 and SSWG1), and social security taxes (SSTax)—give different, but mutually consistent, estimates of the effects of social security on consumption and saving. Table 6 shows the estimated reduction in the 1971 saving–income ratio for each of the regressions. For 1929–1974, the M_2 regressions all imply a reduction of about 25 to 30 percent in the 1971 private saving–income ratio. This is a bit lower than Feldstein's estimate of 38 percent but close to the 26 percent revised estimate based on Feldstein's results. These estimated effects are quite large in an economic sense. However, they are not statistically distinguishable from zero even at a liberal 10 percent level of significance.[29] If one had no other evidence, a 25 to 30 percent reduction in saving is the best estimate. But the imprecision with which the SS_t coefficients are measured is such that it would not be at all surprising to find that the true effect was anywhere from a reduction of 50 percent to an increase of 25 percent.

Against this weak evidence of a substantial reduction in saving because of social security for the period from 1929 to 1974 must be set the results for the postwar period from 1947 to 1974, which are also statistically insignificant and quite inconsistent. In the best-fitting M_1 regressions for this latter period, social security is actually

---

[29] For the M_1 regressions, the estimated effects were a bit higher and statistically significant at the 10 percent level. In the M_2 regressions, the SSW coefficients are statistically significant at the 20 percent level, a marginal improvement relative to Feldstein's estimate of the full equation (5).

TABLE 6

ESTIMATED PERCENTAGE REDUCTION IN THE 1971 SAVING–INCOME RATIO
BECAUSE OF SOCIAL SECURITY

Period and Money Concept	Social Security Scale Variable			
	SSWN1	SSWG1	Barro	SSTax
1929–1974, M_2	28.6[a]	31.6[a]	4.2	25.9[a]
1947–1974, M_1	—37.5	—42.6	4.2	4.0
1929–1974, M_1	34.6[b]	39.5[b]	—15.0	32.6[b]
1947–1974, M_2	4.6	29.0	6.6	6.2

NOTE: Minus indicates an estimated increase.
[a] Significant at 20 percent level.
[b] Significant at 10 percent level.

estimated to reduce consumption and increase saving for Feldstein's social security wealth variables.

The results of these regressions, which show that social security has reduced saving only if the data for the 1930s are included, may be interpreted in two different ways. One is that, in the postwar period, there was so little variation of social security around trend that an effect cannot be detected unless the earlier period of rapid change is included. The other interpretation is that the social security variables serve to divide the overall period into a period of depression and a postwar period of expansion.[30] Changes in the economy, inadequacies in the linear regression in depressions, or problems in prewar/postwar data consistency show up in the estimated coefficient. Barro's results showed that an alternative method of dividing current income into permanent and transitory components (using the unemployment rate) yielded no statistically significant social security effects.

It appears that the estimated effect of social security depends on the method by which current income is divided into permanent and transitory components. If the unemployment rate is used, no significant effect is found. If Friedman's estimator—which may be interpreted as a perpetual inventory of wealth[31]—is used, an economically but not statistically significant reduction in saving is found for the

[30] This does not occur for Barro's coverage x benefit variable, however. The reason is that the zeros for 1929–1936 are offset by high values (about a seventh of the 1970s values) for 1937–1940 for Barro's variable. For the other SS_t variables, the 1937–1940 values average about a twentieth of their 1970s values.
[31] See Michael R. Darby, "The Permanent Income Theory of Consumption—A Restatement," *Quarterly Journal of Economics*, vol. 88 (May 1974), pp. 228–50.

entire period. Those who doubt the existence of a social security effect would argue that the coefficient of transitory income was likely higher during the depression than during postwar years because buffer stocks of liquid assets were exhausted.[32] Since transitory income was negative during the depression, too low a coefficient would overestimate consumption and underestimate saving. This would be offset in the regression estimates by a lower permanent income coefficient and a positive coefficient on SS_t, which is similar to permanent income except during the depression. The permanent income coefficients are lower in each of the 1929–1974 regressions than in the corresponding 1947–1974 regressions.

There is no obvious way to resolve this impasse. The results obtained vary sharply with the consumer expenditure function used and the time periods covered. For the 1929–1974 time period, the regressions indicate a 25 to 30 percent reduction in the saving–income ratio. For the 1947–1974 time period, the effect is essentially nil or even an increase. Although there are good reasons—including the maximal Feldstein-Munnell effects estimated in Chapter 3—to view the 25 to 30 percent reduction as an overestimate of the effect of social security, it might not be. These results could be taken as confirming Feldstein's results in principle, if not in detail. The effect of social security on saving is still an open issue. The reduction in the saving–income ratio is certainly not much larger than 25 percent (if anything, this estimate is biased upward), and it is probably closer to or less than 10 percent.

Appendix: Data Sources

The sources for the data used in the regression estimates in this chapter are reported below. The actual series are reported in Tables 7 through 10. National income accounts data are from the National Bureau of Economic Research (NBER) data bank except as otherwise noted.

SSWG1 Feldstein's gross social security wealth variable computed using a net discount factor of 1.01 as described in Feldstein, "Social Security, Induced Retirement, and Aggregate Capital Accumulation," pp. 914–16. Data through 1961 in billions of 1958 dollars are reported in Munnell, *The Effect of Social*

---

[32] For exactly this argument without reference to social security, see Axel Leijonhufvud, "Effective Demand Failures," *Swedish Journal of Economics*, vol. 75 (1973), pp. 27–48, especially p. 42.

TABLE 7
Data for Alternative Social Security Scale Variables

Year	SSWG1	SSWN1	Barro	SSTax
1929	0.0	0.0	0.0	0.0
1930	0.0	0.0	0.0	0.0
1931	0.0	0.0	0.0	0.0
1932	0.0	0.0	0.0	0.0
1933	0.0	0.0	0.0	0.0
1934	0.0	0.0	0.0	0.0
1935	0.0	0.0	0.0	0.0
1936	0.0	0.0	0.0	0.0
1937	104.000	49.000	33.9425	1.64516
1938	94.000	44.000	30.5037	0.789475
1939	156.000	97.000	34.5390	1.28603
1940	175.000	108.000	37.8529	0.714287
1941	230.000	137.000	42.5819	1.62012
1942	287.000	170.000	41.2132	1.84872
1943	300.000	181.000	36.5366	2.06845
1944	299.000	182.000	33.3813	2.08228
1945	298.000	178.000	33.8485	1.96483
1946	310.000	172.000	37.9488	1.83688
1947	296.000	160.000	35.3108	1.99872
1948	310.000	164.000	34.0184	2.04739
1949	296.000	156.000	33.6866	2.03917
1950	329.000	169.000	42.6535	3.21713
1951	403.000	215.000	70.2160	3.79572
1952	423.000	225.000	71.7279	4.21989
1953	447.000	235.000	83.0854	4.30207
1954	442.000	233.000	86.2457	5.58162
1955	514.000	273.000	109.990	6.15625
1956	552.000	292.000	114.306	6.51055
1957	598.000	313.000	124.345	6.98567
1958	609.000	325.000	123.239	7.56600
1959	658.000	351.000	135.408	7.94868
1960	683.000	367.000	136.894	10.5598

TABLE 7 (continued)

Year	SSWG1	SSWN1	Barro	SSTax
1961	718.000	394.000	140.872	10.8614
1962	799.000	453.000	147.924	11.4957
1963	850.000	485.000	147.438	13.7050
1964	942.700	544.700	149.213	14.6080
1965	1,041.100	600.100	166.654	14.7215
1966	1,149.300	661.300	171.970	18.4574
1967	1,232.300	713.300	170.574	20.2255
1968	1,325.900	770.900	188.483	20.0330
1969	1,406.800	815.800	190.314	22.6292
1970	1,489.800	869.800	210.062	23.3999
1971	1,563.200	922.200	227.510	25.0916
1972	1,688.500	997.500	240.340	27.3974
1973	1,875.200	1,110.200	275.363	31.5114
1974	1,869.900	1,112.900	274.327	32.0499

SOURCES: See text.

TABLE 8
DATA FOR INCOME VARIABLES

Year	Y^{Priv}	Y	Y_P	Y_T
1929	153.121	159.182	159.182	0.0
1930	138.006	144.421	163.230	—18.8085
1931	126.451	132.843	165.856	—33.0128
1932	103.454	109.673	165.993	—56.3200
1933	101.323	107.148	165.869	—58.7208
1934	115.251	120.746	167.112	—46.3664
1935	129.313	134.639	169.664	—35.0256
1936	145.846	151.242	173.710	—22.4680
1937	152.417	158.123	178.179	—20.0561
1938	143.371	149.384	181.483	—32.0988
1939	156.461	162.462	185.879	—23.4167
1940	170.618	176.817	191.423	—14.6060

TABLE 8 (continued)

Year	Y^{Priv}	Y	Y_P	Y_T
1941	177.680	184.239	197.347	—13.1082
1942	184.930	192.000	203.661	—11.6613
1943	192.480	199.296	210.292	—10.9958
1944	200.340	206.814	217.242	—10.4276
1945	208.510	214.633	224.520	—9.88657
1946	217.020	222.966	232.156	—9.18991
1947	225.960	232.657	240.262	—7.60553
1948	243.460	251.148	249.688	1.45963
1949	244.000	252.640	258.648	—6.00790
1950	259.670	269.275	268.687	0.588379
1951	265.770	276.731	278.815	—2.08374
1952	272.810	284.586	289.068	—4.48169
1953	282.120	294.497	299.642	—5.14526
1954	285.460	298.733	309.949	—11.2163
1955	307.210	321.222	321.833	—0.610596
1956	317.000	332.320	334.050	—1.73022
1957	322.480	338.665	346.104	—7.43823
1958	322.810	339.745	357.479	—17.7332
1959	341.290	358.511	369.987	—11.4758
1960	345.780	363.759	382.204	—18.4451
1961	355.630	374.333	394.680	—20.3464
1962	374.700	393.902	408.299	—14.3965
1963	387.310	407.399	422.377	—14.9785
1964	416.860	438.078	438.605	—0.526367
1965	446.710	469.328	456.897	12.4302
1966	471.670	496.115	476.674	19.4402
1967	486.460	512.854	496.834	16.0200
1968	503.970	532.060	517.597	14.4624
1969	512.470	542.701	538.069	4.63159
1970	528.423	560.787	559.013	1.77368
1971	553.835	587.773	581.288	6.48560
1972	581.954	617.933	605.124	12.8098
1973	620.514	659.225	631.532	27.6929
1974	597.481	639.282	654.223	—14.9402

SOURCES: See text.

TABLE 9
Data for Alternative Money Stock Measures

Year	M_1	M_2
1929	47.7397	83.5444
1930	47.3881	84.1419
1931	49.4781	87.0565
1932	48.6998	82.2696
1933	48.0296	75.8621
1934	49.4253	76.7817
1935	57.4325	86.4866
1936	65.3244	100.671
1937	64.5162	96.7743
1938	65.7896	98.4650
1939	74.5012	107.982
1940	85.7144	119.780
1941	94.2506	126.900
1942	100.730	129.380
1943	120.701	150.251
1944	134.810	169.146
1945	151.529	193.884
1946	150.355	196.312
1947	143.517	187.420
1948	136.452	179.952
1949	136.108	180.539
1950	137.636	181.906
1951	134.537	176.524
1952	138.343	182.210
1953	139.913	186.587
1954	140.865	191.568
1955	144.828	197.953
1956	143.460	197.047
1957	139.918	196.315
1958	138.400	201.200
1959	141.856	207.700
1960	139.456	206.511

TABLE 9 (continued)

Year	M_1	M_2
1961	141.001	215.207
1962	142.707	225.644
1963	145.241	237.418
1964	149.162	249.442
1965	153.585	265.717
1966	156.682	279.372
1967	158.829	293.269
1968	164.189	308.531
1969	167.288	315.709
1970	166.976	328.616
1971	172.024	361.012
1972	178.100	363.597
1973	180.740	376.423
1974	171.508	367.077

SOURCES: See text.

TABLE 10
DATA FOR REMAINING VARIABLES IN THE CONSUMER EXPENDITURE FUNCTION

Year	D	C	P_D/P_{ND}	i
1928	60.6080	...	...	...
1929	64.1530	139.600	1.05860	3.60000
1930	63.9180	130.400	1.03600	3.29000
1931	62.1890	126.100	1.02610	3.34000
1932	58.2490	114.800	1.02270	3.68000
1933	54.9500	112.800	1.03460	3.31000
1934	53.2570	118.100	1.03110	3.12000
1935	53.9580	125.500	0.98040	2.79000
1936	57.0610	138.400	0.97150	2.65000
1937	60.1310	143.100	0.98390	2.68000
1938	60.0100	140.200	1.02520	2.56000
1939	61.9900	148.200	1.02220	2.36000
1940	65.5930	155.700	1.02490	2.21000

TABLE 10 (continued)

Year	D	C	P_D/P_{ND}	i
1941	70.6970	165.400	1.03960	2.05000
1942	68.1630	161.400	1.08850	2.46000
1943	64.7430	165.800	1.07680	2.47000
1944	61.2330	171.400	1.14070	2.48000
1945	59.4590	183.000	1.17180	2.37000
1946	66.9670	203.500	1.10110	2.19000
1947	76.8810	206.300	1.07087	2.25000
1948	86.4030	212.300	1.05589	2.44000
1949	96.0570	216.500	1.07258	2.31000
1950	109.617	230.500	1.07048	2.32000
1951	117.768	232.800	1.07440	2.57000
1952	123.774	239.400	1.06247	2.68000
1953	132.735	250.500	1.03290	2.94000
1954	140.125	255.700	1.00532	2.55000
1955	153.198	274.200	0.988406	2.84000
1956	161.856	281.400	1.00135	3.08000
1957	169.360	287.200	1.00898	3.47000
1958	172.216	290.100	0.999576	3.43000
1959	179.790	307.300	1.00149	4.07000
1960	187.041	316.100	0.977200	4.01000
1961	192.024	322.500	0.962749	3.90000
1962	200.895	338.400	0.953963	3.95000
1963	212.188	352.900	0.936349	4.00000
1964	226.180	373.700	0.924064	4.15000
1965	244.449	397.700	0.900126	4.21000
1966	263.941	418.100	0.863988	4.66000
1967	280.902	428.600	0.855488	4.85000
1968	302.313	452.700	0.848809	5.25000
1969	323.641	469.300	0.832743	6.10000
1970	339.380	478.400	0.815279	6.59000
1971	359.800	496.300	0.805295	5.74000
1972	387.110	529.700	0.781104	5.63000
1973	418.020	554.400	0.745972	6.30000
1974	433.720	545.100	0.721284	6.99000

SOURCES: See text.

Security on Personal Saving, p. 126. Anthony J. Pellechio, Feldstein's research assistant, provided revised data from 1962 through 1974.

SSWN1   Feldstein's net social security wealth variable corresponding to SSWG1. It is computed by subtracting from SSWG1 the present value of expected social security taxes to be paid by those currently in the labor force. The sources for the data are the same as for SSWG1.

Barro   An aggregate version of Barro's coverage times benefits variable. This series is given as 1958 dollars per person in Barro, *The Impact of Social Security on Private Saving*. Barro's data are aggregated by multiplying by total population including armed forces overseas (from U.S. Bureau of the Census, *Historical Statistics of the United States, Colonial Times to 1970*, p. 8; and *Economic Report of the President, January 1977*, p. 217) in billions to obtain aggregate data in billions of 1958 dollars.

SSTax   Net total contributions to the Old-Age and Survivors Insurance Trust Fund (from the *Social Security Bulletin, Annual Statistical Supplement*, 1974, p. 62) divided by the implicit price deflator for personal consumption expenditures to obtain billions of 1958 dollars.

Y^{Priv} Private sector income divided by the implicit price deflator for personal consumption expenditures to obtain billions of 1958 dollars. Nominal private sector income measures all income of the private sector whether received in cash or accrued. For a complete discussion, see Michael R. Darby, *Macroeconomics: The Theory of Income, Employment, and the Price Level* (New York: McGraw-Hill Book Co., 1976), p. 20.

Y Measured income defined as real private sector income adjusted for the imputed yield on the stock of consumers' durable goods (in billions of 1958 dollars), where D_t is the real stock of durable goods at the end of year t (see below),

$$Y_t = Y_t^{Priv} + 0.1 \, D_{t-1}.$$

Y_p Permanent income in billions of 1958 dollars. This is computed by the exponentially declining weight method as:

$$Y_{Pt} = \beta Y_t + (1 - \beta)(1 + g)Y_{Pt-1},$$

where β is 0.1, g is the period's trend growth rate of 0.0386 per annum, and $Y_{P,1929} = Y_{1929}$. The latter assumption was made because an initial value estimated from a trend regression is unduly depressed by the Depression. The real income data for 1941–1946 were replaced by a log-linear interpolation from 1940 to 1947 to alleviate problems in the data for the war years. These years were not used in the regressions, but only to obtain $Y_{P,1947}$. The reported conclusions are unchanged (although the $\bar{R}^2$'s of the regressions decline) if the reported war year Y's or the war year Y's estimated from a time trend regression are used. For further discussion of the calculation of permanent income, see Darby, "The Consumer Expenditure Function," p. 652.

Y_T Transitory income in billions of 1958 dollars, $Y_{Tt} = Y_t - Y_{Pt}$.

M_1 Money supply M_1 (average of monthly data in the NBER data bank) divided by the implicit price deflator for personal consumption expenditures to obtain billions of 1958 dollars.

M_2 Money supply M_2 (average of monthly data in the NBER data bank) divided by the implicit price deflator for personal consumption expenditures to obtain billions of 1958 dollars.

D Stock of consumers' durable goods at the end of the year in billions of 1958 dollars. This stock is estimated as a perpetual inventory by:

$$D_t = 0.904282C_t^d + 0.8145D_{t-1},$$

where C^d is real personal consumption expenditures for durable goods. Data from 1946 on are from Darby, "The Consumer Expenditure Function," p. 666. These data were extended backward from the 1946 benchmark by inverting the inventory equation.

C Personal consumption expenditures in billions of 1958 dollars.

62

P_D/P_{ND} Relative price of durable to nondurable goods and services computed by dividing the implicit price deflator for personal consumption expenditures on durable goods by the implicit price deflator for personal consumption expenditures on nondurable goods and services.

i Yield to maturity for long-term U.S. government bonds from the NBER data bank.

5

Integration of Saving and Labor Force Effects on Income and the Capital Stock

The long-run effects of social security on American income and the capital stock depend upon the role of the United States in the world economy. If the United States is viewed as insulated from the rest of the world by effective controls on capital flows, it would be a closed economy. If, on the other hand, it is seen as a small part of a large world capital market, it is best characterized as a "small open economy." In fact, the U.S. economy falls between those extreme cases—it is somewhat open to capital flows and is a significant factor in the world capital market. Nevertheless, in order to determine the effects of social security, it is useful to examine the two polar cases.

In a closed economy in the long run, income and the capital stock are affected by changes in both the saving–income ratio and the supply of labor induced by the social security program. Chapters 2–4 examined the effect of social security on the saving–income ratio. In this chapter, the results of those chapters are combined with other research results on the labor supply effect. The income and capital effects are computed for a number of alternative combinations of the saving–income ratio and the labor supply effects.

In a small open economy, the effects of social security are not difficult to calculate, although the distinction between the income of residents of the United States (NNP) and the output in the United States (NDP) becomes important. For these calculations, the effects are also computed for alternative combinations of saving–income and labor supply effects.

The Effects in a Closed Economy

The long-run equilibrium of the economy can be characterized as one of balanced or steady-state growth. Under such conditions, income and the capital stock grow at the same rate as the supply of labor. The growth of labor supply results from growth in population, hours worked per capita, education and training, and technological innovation. In a closed economy, growth in capital is determined by the amount of domestic saving available to finance investment. Income grows because of the growth in the basic factors of production—labor and capital.

The Neoclassical Growth Model. Long-run growth equilibrium may be analyzed using a simple neoclassical growth model.[1] The labor supply (L_t) measured in efficiency units is assumed to grow at a constant rate of g per annum continuously compounded as shown in equation (7):

$$L_t = L_0 e^{gt}, \tag{7}$$

where L_0 is the labor supply at time 0. The model is completed by assuming a linear homogeneous (constant-returns-to-scale) aggregate production function as shown in equation (8):

$$Y_t = f(K_t, L_t), \tag{8}$$

and a constant saving–income ratio as shown in equation (9):

$$\frac{dK_t}{dt} = \dot{K}_t = \sigma Y_t. \tag{9}$$

In equation (9), Y_t is the level of real income and output, K_t is the capital stock, and $\dot{K}_t$ is the rate of change in the capital stock (investment).[2]

The growth rate of the capital stock is obtained by dividing equation (9) by K_t:

$$\frac{\dot{K}_t}{K_t} = \sigma \frac{Y_t}{K_t}. \tag{10}$$

Substituting equation (8) and simplifying produces equation (11):

$$\frac{\dot{K}_t}{K_t} = \sigma f(1, L_t/K_t). \tag{11}$$

The growth rate of the capital stock is an increasing function of the labor–capital ratio. Figure 13 graphs equation (11) together with the

---

[1] For more complete expositions of this model, see Robert M. Solow, *Growth Theory: An Exposition* (Oxford: Oxford University Press, 1970), pp. 1–38; and Michael R. Darby, *Macroeconomics: The Theory of Income, Employment, and the Price Level* (New York: McGraw-Hill, 1976), pp. 112–21.

[2] Note that government and private accounts are consolidated so that σ is the fraction of income available to finance investment.

FIGURE 13

Determination of Equilibrium Labor-Capital Ratio in the Simple Neoclassical Growth Model

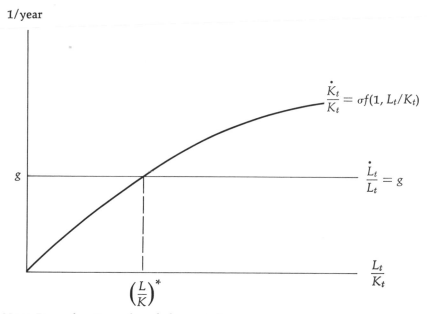

1/year

$$\frac{\dot{K}_t}{K_t} = \sigma f(1, L_t/K_t)$$

$$\frac{\dot{L}_t}{L_t} = g$$

g

$\left(\frac{L}{K}\right)^*$

$\frac{L_t}{K_t}$

NOTE: For explanations of symbols, see text.

growth rate of labor (g). Since the growth rate of labor exceeds the growth rate of capital for L_t/K_t less than $(L/K)^*$ and vice versa for L_t/K_t greater than $(L/K)^*$, the labor–capital ratio will move toward and remain at $(L/K)^*$. This long-run equilibrium value determines the equilibrium capital stock given equation (7) and hence the equilibrium income given equation (8).[3]

Figure 14 plots the moving equilibrium values of income, the capital stock, and the labor supply on a graph with a vertical ratio scale. Each variable grows at the constant growth rate of labor (g).[4] **Equilibrium Effects of Social Security.** The social security program affects income and the capital stock in the closed economy through two of the proximate determinants of the growth equilibrium: the saving–income ratio and the labor supply.

---

[3] Note that $Y_t/L_t = f(K_t/L_t, 1)$ so the $(K/L)^* \equiv 1/(L/K)^*$ determines a unique equilibrium income–labor ratio $(Y/L)^*$.

[4] This growth rate is indicated by the (identical) slopes of the growth paths of the variables. Note that per capita income grows to the extent that the growth rate of labor measured in efficiency units exceeds the growth rate of population.

FIGURE 14

Income, Capital Stock, and Labor
Supply Growth in the Simple Neoclassical Growth Model

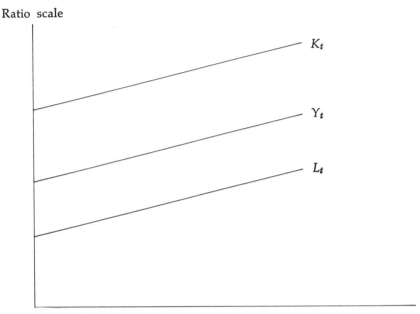

Ratio scale

K_t

Y_t

L_t

Time

Note: For explanations of symbols, see text.

The change in the saving–income ratio induced by social security is ambiguous in theory, but the empirical results discussed in Chapters 3 and 4 suggest that this ratio either remains unchanged or decreases. In the following discussion, a circumflex denotes values with social security; thus:

$$\hat{\sigma} \leq \sigma. \tag{12}$$

Induced retirement causes a once-and-for-all decrease in the average hours worked per capita. This reduces the quantity of labor at any time to a fraction λ of what it would otherwise be. There is no reason for the growth rate of labor supply (g) to be affected except during the transitional period of rising retirement. Thus, the labor supply with social security is given by:

$$\hat{L}_t = \lambda L_0 e^{gt}, \tag{13}$$

where $\lambda < 1$.

FIGURE 15

COMPARISON OF INCOME, CAPITAL STOCK, AND LABOR SUPPLY WITH AND
WITHOUT SOCIAL SECURITY WITH NO CHANGE IN THE
SAVING-INCOME RATIO

Ratio scale

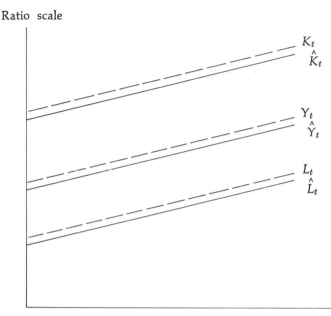

Time

NOTE: For explanations of symbols, see text.

If the saving–income ratio is not affected by social security
($\hat{\sigma} = \sigma$), the equilibrium labor–capital ratio in Figure 13 is unchanged.
Since income and capital are proportional to labor, both are reduced
in proportion to the fall in labor:

$$\hat{K}_t = \lambda K_t; \tag{14}$$

$$\hat{Y}_t = \lambda Y_t. \tag{15}$$

This result is illustrated in Figure 15, in which the solid lines for the
variables with social security are lower than but parallel to the broken
lines for the variables without social security.

If the saving–income ratio falls ($\sigma < \sigma$) as argued by Feldstein,
the analysis is somewhat more complicated. Figure 16 shows that the
fall in the saving–income ratio implies that the capital–labor ratio will
also fall.[5] At the lower capital–labor ratio, income per efficiency unit

---

[5] That is, the labor–capital ratio will rise.

FIGURE 16

Effect on the Labor-Capital Ratio of a Fall in the Saving-Income Ratio Induced by Social Security

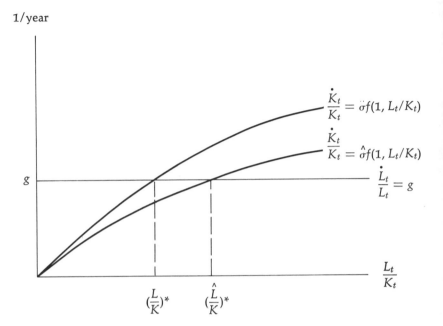

NOTE: For explanations of symbols, see text.

of labor will also fall. The growth rates of capital and income will be unaffected, however, except during the period of adjustment to the new equilibrium.

For the United States, the capital stock per labor unit will fall by a greater percentage and income per labor unit by a smaller percentage than the fall in the saving–income ratio.[6] If income per labor unit with

---

[6] For small changes in σ, with a given growth path of labor, and with labor's share of total income denoted as α, it can be shown that: (a) the capital stock falls by x/α percent if the saving–income ratio falls by x percent ($\frac{d \log K}{d \log \sigma} = 1/\alpha$); and (b) real income falls by $x(\frac{1}{\alpha} - 1)$ percent if the saving–income ratio falls by x percent ($\frac{d \log Y}{d \log \sigma} = \frac{1}{\alpha} - 1$). For the United States, α is about 0.75; thus, a 10 percent decline in σ (for example, from 0.10 to 0.09) would cause the capital stock per labor unit to fall by about 13⅓ percent and real income to fall by about 3⅓ percent.

social security is a fraction μ of what it would be without social security,[7] then the combined effect of the fall in the saving–income ratio and in labor supply on the long-run equilibrium values of capital stock and income is given by:

$$\hat{K}_t = \frac{\hat{\sigma}}{\sigma} \mu\lambda K_t; \tag{16}$$

$$\hat{Y}_t = \mu\lambda Y_t. \tag{17}$$

Thus, the capital stock falls more than in proportion to the fall in the saving–income ratio because of the fall in income resulting from the reduced labor supply and capital stock. Figure 17 illustrates the alternative long-run equilibrium growth paths of the capital stock, income, and labor supply with and without social security under these conditions.

Alternative Estimated Effects in a Closed Economy. The formulas derived above can be used to estimate the effects of social security in a closed economy.[8] Unfortunately, because there is no agreement on the appropriate reductions in the labor supply and the saving–income ratio, calculations must be made for the whole range of alternative values suggested in the research done on this subject.

Estimates of labor force effects. The social security program may affect the labor supply both through induced retirement and through changes in the preretirement labor supply. The limited research that has been done has concentrated on estimating the magnitude of the induced retirement effects.

Michael Boskin has analyzed the effects of social security on retirement.[9] His study shows the crucial impact of the high implicit tax rate in the earnings test on inducing retirement. A naive reading of Boskin's regressions (in which increases in the earnings of either the worker or a spouse reduce the probability of retirement) would

---

[7] Carrying forward the argument of note 6 above, μ would be approximated by $1 + \frac{\hat{\sigma} - \sigma}{\sigma} (\frac{1}{\alpha} - 1)$ for small changes in σ. If in fact $\hat{\sigma} = \sigma$, $\mu = 1$ and equations (16) and (17) reduce to equations (14) and (15).

[8] A degree of approximation is introduced by computing μ as indicated in note 7 above for other than small changes in σ. This would not seem to be a serious problem since the U.S. aggregate production function seems to be well approximated by the Cobb-Douglas form $Y = AK_t^{(1-\alpha)} L_t^\alpha$, in which labor's share α is constant and about 0.75.

[9] Michael J. Boskin, "Social Security and Retirement Decisions," *Economic Inquiry*, vol. 15 (January 1977), pp. 1–25.

FIGURE 17

COMPARISON OF INCOME, CAPITAL STOCK, AND LABOR SUPPLY WITH AND
WITHOUT SOCIAL SECURITY WITH CHANGE IN THE SAVING-INCOME RATIO

Ratio scale

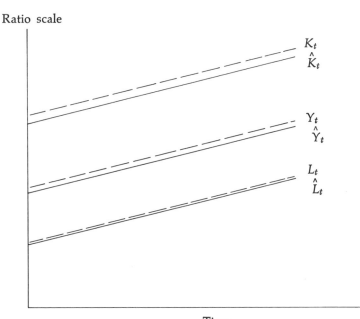

Time

NOTE: For explanations of symbols, see text.

suggest that the labor force participation of the elderly would have
increased over time in the absence of social security. However, the
negative coefficient on a worker's own earnings may be caused by
the operation of the earnings test in the cross-section sample. Accord-
ing to Boskin's results, social security has accelerated the downward
trend in labor force participation of elderly men, but his results give
no reliable indication of by how much.

A recent survey article by Colin and Rosemary Campbell also
found the weight of evidence to support the conclusion that OASI has
accelerated the decline in labor force participation of elderly men.[10]
The range of these effects, however, is rather limited. Feldstein
calculated that, "if the labor force participation rates of those over

[10] Colin D. Campbell and Rosemary G. Campbell, "Conflicting Views on the
Effect of Old-Age and Survivors Insurance on Retirement," *Economic Inquiry*,
vol. 14 (September 1976), pp. 369–88.

65 were at the 1930 values, the labor force in 1970 would be increased by less than 3 percent."[11]

To my knowledge, no studies have been made of the effects of social security on the preretirement supply of labor.[12] The total effect of social security on the preretirement supply of labor combines four different effects. First, there is a negative substitution effect because a dollar in social security taxes increases the present value of future benefits by less than a dollar.[13] As a result, net wages are reduced and leisure is cheaper. Second, to the extent that the lump-sum minimum benefit does not make up for the wealth loss in taxes paid, wealth and leisure are reduced and the labor supply is increased. This positive wealth effect occurs if the real interest rate used in making life-cycle plans exceeds the implicit yield on social security (about 3.25 percent a year). Third, a positive wealth effect also results from the reduced income caused by induced retirement. Finally, a positive intertemporal substitution effect may exist in which people substitute leisure during induced retirement for leisure during the preretirement years.

The third and fourth effects would partially offset the reduction in the labor supply resulting from induced retirement, but would leave a residual negative impact. The first and second effects can be thought of as the net effect of a wage reduction partially compensated for by a lump-sum benefit. It is usually argued that the supply of labor is backward-bending with respect to uncompensated wage changes; that is, lower wages are associated with increased labor supply. The partial lump-sum compensation works in the opposite direction, and there can be no presumption of a net decrease or increase in preretirement labor supply from the first two effects combined.

Overall, social security probably reduces the total supply of labor somewhere in the range from 0 to 3 percent. However, this range is questionable, given the lack of evidence that the net preretirement effect is small.

Estimates of the effects on the saving–income ratio. The range of estimates of the reduction in the saving–income ratio range from

---

[11] Martin Feldstein, "Social Security, Induced Retirement, and Aggregate Capital Accumulation," p. 924. Since the elderly appear to be below the average for the population in labor efficiency units per capita, this is probably a doubly safe upper limit on the reduction in labor supply resulting from induced retirement.

[12] Michael J. Boskin, Michael D. Hurd, and Lawrence J. Lau of Stanford University are currently engaged in a major study of the effects of social security on labor supply.

[13] This results from the large welfare element in the minimum benefit that is currently received by everyone who pays a trivial amount of taxes for forty calendar quarters.

Barro's 0 to Feldstein's 38 percent. In Chapter 4, however, it was shown that Feldstein's estimate of 38 percent exaggerates the impact, and his studies indicate a reduction of about 26 percent. Munnell estimated a reduction of about 5 percent.[14] My own time series estimates, presented in Chapter 4, suggest a reduction from 0 to 30 percent.

The empirical results to date have not come up with any clear-cut answer. It appears probable that some reduction in the saving–income ratio has occurred. For the calculations below, the following percentage reductions will be used: 0, 2.5, 5.0, 7.5, 10.0, 15.0, 20.0, 26.0, and 38.0 percent. The results for the range from 0 to 10.0 percent are probably the most significant.

Combined closed-economy effects. The combined effects in a closed economy of labor supply and saving–income ratio reductions for income and the capital stock are shown in Tables 11 and 12, respectively.[15]

Table 11 indicates that, in a closed economy, induced reductions in the saving–income ratio as small as 10 percent have substantial effects on real income. These income effects are substantial since OASI benefits are about 4 percent of the net national product. Suppose, for example, that the saving–income ratio falls from 0.111 to 0.100—a 10 percent reduction—because of social security. This would imply a fall in income of from 3.3 percent to 6.2 percent and a fall in total and per capita consumption of from 2.3 percent to 5.2 percent. The latter calculation takes into account the higher (private and government) consumption implied by the lower saving–income ratio. Partially offsetting the reduction in consumption would be the value of the "forced" leisure represented by the induced reduction in the labor supply.

As can be seen in Table 12, the interaction of the reductions in income, the capital stock, and the labor supply result in larger reductions in the capital stock than would be predicted from the fall in the saving–income ratio alone. Plausible values of social security effects yield substantial reductions—from 5 to 20 percent—in the capital stock in a closed economy, but these reductions are smaller than Feldstein's original estimate.

---

[14] Alicia H. Munnell, "The Impact of Social Security on Personal Savings," *National Tax Journal*, vol. 27 (December 1974), p. 562. Munnell estimated a $2.9 billion reduction in personal saving for 1969. It is assumed that this reduction is reflected in private saving of $53.4 billion for 1969.

[15] For these calculations, it is assumed that labor's share α is 0.75.

TABLE 11
PERCENTAGE REDUCTIONS IN REAL INCOME
IN A CLOSED ECONOMY

Percentage Reduction in the Saving–Income Ratio	Percentage Reduction in Labor Supply		
	0.0 percent	1.5 percent	3.0 percent
0.0	0.0	1.5	3.0
2.5	0.8	2.3	3.8
5.0	1.7	3.1	4.6
7.5	2.5	4.0	5.4
10.0	3.3	4.8	6.2
15.0	5.0	6.4	7.9
20.0	6.7	8.1	9.5
26.0	8.7	10.0	11.4
38.0	12.7	14.0	15.3

TABLE 12
PERCENTAGE REDUCTIONS IN THE CAPITAL STOCK
IN A CLOSED ECONOMY

Percentage Reduction in the Saving–Income Ratio	Percentage Reduction in Labor Supply		
	0.0 percent	1.5 percent	3.0 percent
0.0	0.0	1.5	3.0
2.5	3.3	4.8	6.2
5.0	6.6	8.0	9.4
7.5	9.8	11.2	12.5
10.0	13.0	14.3	15.6
15.0	19.2	20.5	21.7
20.0	25.3	26.5	27.6
26.0	32.4	33.4	34.4
38.0	45.9	46.7	47.5

The Case of a Small Open Economy

The other polar case is that of the small open economy in which capital flows freely to and from the rest of the world. For the world as a whole, the neoclassical growth model would be applicable with only minor modifications. That is, the world saving–income ratio, growth rate of labor, and aggregate production function would determine an equilibrium capital–labor ratio. Capital would flow from countries with relatively high saving–income ratios to those with relatively low saving–income ratios, thus equating the returns to capital and labor (measured in efficiency units) throughout the world.[16] The amount of capital used in any country would be proportional to the amount of its labor.

What will be the effects of social security in a small open economy?[17] Because the country is small, any reduction in its saving–income ratio would have a negligible effect on the world supply of saving or the capital–labor ratio. The capital stock within the country would fall only in proportion to the induced fall in labor supply. A reduction in the saving–income ratio would reduce the amount of capital *owned* by residents of the country, whether that capital is located at home or abroad. A sufficient fall, for example, might cause the country to shift from being a net creditor to being a net debtor.

A Formal Analysis. It is necessary to distinguish between the output produced by the factors of production located within the country regardless of by whom owned—the net domestic product (NDP)— and the income received by the country's residents regardless of where earned—the net national product (NNP). Total income (NNP) is denoted by Y_t. Net domestic product (NDP) is denoted by Q_t. The difference between Y_t and Q_t is the yield on net foreign securities held (rF_t).[18]

Because the ratio of output to labor is fixed by the constant world capital–labor ratio, the introduction of social security would reduce

---

[16] It is presumed, however, that saving–income ratios are based on income inclusive of returns on foreign investments or net of foreign loans. This complicates the determination of the equilibrium because the world saving–income ratio is endogenous.

[17] For descriptions of growth in open economies, see James A. Hanson and Phillip A. Neher, "The Neoclassical Theorem Once Again: Closed and Open Economies," *American Economic Review*, vol. 57 (September 1967), pp. 869–79; and Phillip A. Neher, *Economic Growth and Development: A Mathematical Introduction* (New York: John Wiley and Sons, 1971), pp. 257–82.

[18] If the nation were a net debtor, F_t would be negative and income would be less than output because of net interest payments to foreigners.

the long-run equilibrium output and the supply of capital in proportion to the fall in the labor supply, regardless of any effects on the saving–income ratio: [19]

$$\hat{K}_t = \lambda K_t; \tag{18}$$

$$\hat{Q}_t = \lambda Q_t. \tag{19}$$

The long-run equilibrium level of income and the total amount of capital $(K_t + F_t)$ owned by the country's residents would be affected further if the saving–income ratio fell. Using μ for the ratio of income per labor unit with social security to income per labor unit without social security,[20] the combined effect on owned capital and income is given by:

$$\hat{K}_t + \hat{F}_t = \frac{\hat{\sigma}}{\sigma} \mu\lambda(K_t + F_t); \tag{20}$$

$$\hat{Y}_t = \mu\lambda Y_t. \tag{21}$$

In sum, the capital stock used and the output produced fall only in proportion to the induced fall in the supply of labor in a small open economy. The capital stock owned and the income received by the residents of the country fall further, however, if the saving–income ratio is reduced by social security.

Combined Open-Economy Effects. The total (and per capita) output and used capital stock fall in proportion to the induced reduction in the labor supply. This reduction has been estimated at between 0 and 3 percent.

Total (and per capita) income and capital stock owned fall further as indicated by equations (20) and (21). Tables 13 and 14 compute the approximate effects implied by various combinations of induced

---

[19] See note 3 above.

[20] For small changes in σ and a given growth path of labor, it can be shown that: the owned capital stock falls by $x(1 + \frac{\sigma r}{g - \sigma r})$ percent if the saving–income ratio falls by x percent $(\frac{d \log(K + F)}{d \log \sigma} = 1 + \frac{\sigma r}{g - \sigma r})$; and real income falls by $x \frac{\sigma r}{g - \sigma r}$ percent if the saving–income ratio falls by x percent $(\frac{d \log Y}{d \log \sigma} = \frac{\sigma r}{g - \sigma r})$. If g is 0.0325 a year and σ is about 0.1, then a 10 percent decline in σ would cause owned capital to fall by 11.0, 12.3, or 13.8 percent, depending on whether a 3, 6, or 9 percent a year interest rate r is assumed. The corresponding reductions in income are 1.0, 2.3, or 3.8 percent, respectively.

reductions in labor supply and the saving–income ratio. The calculations are based on values in the United States of the parameters and an assumed real interest rate of 3 percent a year.[21]

Table 13 shows that income would be reduced less than under similar conditions in a closed economy. For example, a 10 percent reduction in the saving–income ratio in a small open economy reduces income per unit of labor by 1.1 percent as compared with 3.3 percent in a closed economy (see Table 11). Further, this result is dependent on the interest rate used. At a rate of 3 percent a year, the fall in income because of a smaller owned capital stock is relatively trivial. At higher interest rates, the loss is larger. For example, at a 9 percent interest rate, the same 10 percent reduction in the saving–income ratio would cause a 4.1 percent reduction in income in an open economy instead of a 1.1 percent reduction. Of course, higher interest rates would also imply smaller values of net social security wealth and therefore smaller reductions in the saving–income ratio.

TABLE 13
Percentage Reductions in Real Income in a Small Open Economy

Percentage Reduction in the Saving–Income Ratio	Percentage Reduction in Labor Supply		
	0.0 percent	1.5 percent	3.0 percent
0.0	0.0	1.5	3.0
2.5	0.3	1.8	3.3
5.0	0.5	2.0	3.5
7.5	0.8	2.3	3.8
10.0	1.1	2.6	4.0
15.0	1.7	3.1	4.6
20.0	2.3	3.8	5.2
26.0	3.2	4.6	6.1
38.0	5.2	6.6	8.1

[21] That is, g is assumed to be 0.0325, $\hat{\sigma}$ is approximated by 0.10 (government and private saving rates taken as equal), and σ is implied by the assumed percentage reduction. The value of μ is calculated as $\mu = 1 - \frac{\sigma - \hat{\sigma}}{\sigma} \left(\frac{\bar{\sigma} r}{g - \bar{\sigma} r} \right)$, where $\bar{\sigma} = (\hat{\sigma} + \sigma)/2$.

TABLE 14

PERCENTAGE REDUCTIONS IN THE OWNED CAPIT/
STOCK IN A SMALL OPEN ECONOMY

Percentage Reduction in the Saving–Income Ratio	Percentage Reduction in Labor Supply		
	0.0 percent	1.5 percent	3.0 percent
0.0	0.0	1.5	3.0
2.5	2.7	4.2	5.7
5.0	5.5	6.9	8.3
7.5	8.2	9.6	10.1
10.0	11.1	12.3	13.6
15.0	16.4	17.7	18.9
20.0	21.9	23.0	24.2
26.0	28.3	29.4	30.5
38.0	41.2	42.1	43.0

Summing up the Combined Effects

The United States falls somewhere between the two polar cases of a closed economy and a small open economy. The capital stock used and the output produced in the United States would fall more than in proportion to the induced fall in the supply of labor if the saving–income ratio were also reduced. But this fall would be less than the reduction in both the capital stock owned and the income received by U.S. residents because part of the effect of the fall in the saving–income ratio would be to reduce net U.S. holdings of foreign securities.

The combined effect of social security probably has been to reduce the owned capital stock from 5 to 20 percent. The used capital stock may not be reduced at all, but a decrease of up to 15 percent would not be implausible. The corresponding reductions in income and output range from 2 percent to 7 percent and from 0 percent to 4 percent, respectively. These broad ranges reflect the inconclusive state of empirical research on social security.

6

Conclusions

The research reported in this study emphasizes the complex nature and uncertain magnitudes of the effects of social security on the capital stock and income. Nonetheless, some substantial progress has been made.

The first finding is that using the zero-bequest life-cycle model to explain aggregate saving and capital holdings has serious limitations. The bulk of capital is held and net saving is made in anticipation of bequests. Social security would cause saving for bequests, relative to income, to fall only to the extent that the forced "purchase" of a life annuity exceeds what would otherwise be purchased and thus reduces the precautionary value of bequest assets.

Social security, however, may have greatly reduced life-cycle saving. Because bequest saving is relatively stable, the percentage effect of social security on total saving is much less than on life-cycle saving alone. Even so, the possible reduction in total saving because of reduced life-cycle saving is still large—12 percent to 23 percent, depending on the interest rate—although these estimates are less than Feldstein's original 38 percent reduction. This maximum reduction would be offset by the effects of induced retirement, the low effective yield on social security, and the uncertainty of benefits.

Since the retirement effect alone apparently swamps the possible reduction in bequest saving relative to income, the reduction in the total private saving–income ratio is probably no more than 10 percent to 25 percent. Time series estimates of the effect of social security on saving imply a reduction ranging from 0 to about 30 percent. The higher estimates depend on the functional form and time period used in the estimation and are probably biased upward. None of the estimated reductions differ significantly from zero on standard statistical sts. Taken as a whole, the evidence suggests that the reduction in the saving–income ratio because of social security is probably from 0 to 10 percent rather than higher.

A second finding is that, because the U.S. capital market is relatively open internationally, the capital stock owned by U.S. residents wherever located should be distinguished from that used in the United States by whomever owned. Similarly, the income of U.S. residents (NNP) should be distinguished from the output of the United States (NDP). In the long run, reductions in the saving–income ratio and the labor supply will reduce the capital owned and the income received by U.S. residents more than the capital used and the output produced in the United States.

Calculations of the long-run equilibrium effects suggest that owned capital is reduced from 5 percent to 20 percent and used capital from 0 percent to 15 percent. The corresponding reductions in income and output range from 2 percent to 7 percent and from 0 percent to 4 percent, respectively.

In 1974, OASI taxes and benefits were close to 5 percent of the net national product. The estimates made in this study suggest a total tax plus income burden of $1.40 to $2.40 for each dollar of OASI benefits. Offsetting this excess burden would be any value of the increased leisure implicit in the induced retirement and any rise in consumption relative to income.

It is deceptively easy to look at the implied reductions in capital and income and to conclude that something must be done to the social security program. This involves giant steps over two unresolved questions: First, is the reduction in capital and income good or bad? Second, if it is bad, are changes in the social security program the best way to eliminate these reductions? This study does not provide answers to either of these questions, although it might be used in analyzing them.

Martin Feldstein has pointed out that the welfare implications of the reductions in the capital stock induced by social security cannot be analyzed in isolation.[1] An important issue is whether the aggregate capital stock is too small or too large. Evidence that social security reduces the capital stock is of interest primarily because changes in social security would then be included among the possible policy tools to increase (or decrease) a capital stock that is currently too small (large).

---

[1] Martin S. Feldstein, "Does the United States Save Too Little?" *American Economic Review, Papers and Proceedings*, vol. 67 (February 1977), pp. 116–21.

Proposals to fund the social security system over a short period of time are the same as proposals to run a large government surplus, thus inducing "forced saving."[2] If such a surplus were desired, it is not obvious why the surplus should be tied to social security or why tying it to social security would alter the amount available to finance investment in capital goods.

Policy tools other than a government surplus are also available to encourage private saving and investment. An important example is changes in tax laws that could have major effects on increasing the capital stock.

Other important issues—such as the effect on the economic well-being of the elderly, the burden of the taxes, the forced participation, and induced retirement—are also basic to an overall evaluation of the social security system.

---

[2] The idea is that, if private saving falls by less than the increase in taxes to finance the surplus, the amount available to finance private investment will increase. Whether this does or does not occur is not a settled issue.

BIBLIOGRAPHY

Aaron, Henry. "Social Security: International Comparisons." In *Studies in the Economics of Income Maintenance*, edited by Otto Eckstein. Washington, D.C.: Brookings Institution, 1967.

Ando, Albert, and Modigliani, Franco. "The 'Life Cycle' Hypothesis of Saving: Aggregate Implications and Tests." *American Economic Review*, March 1963, 53: 55–84.

Barro, Robert J. "Are Government Bonds Net Wealth?" *Journal of Political Economy*, July/August 1974, 82: 1095–1117.

————. *The Impact of Social Security on Private Saving: Evidence from the U.S. Time Series.* Washington, D.C.: American Enterprise Institute, 1978.

Blinder, Alan S. "Intergenerational Transfers and Life Cycle Consumption." *American Economic Review, Papers and Proceedings*, May 1976, 66: 87–93.

Boskin, Michael J. "Social Security and Retirement Decisions." *Economic Inquiry*, January 1977, 15: 1–25.

Browning, Edgar K. "Social Insurance and Intergenerational Transfers." *Journal of Law and Economics*, October 1973, 16: 215–37.

Campbell, Colin D., and Campbell, Rosemary G. "Conflicting Views on the Effect of Old-Age and Survivors Insurance on Retirement." *Economic Inquiry*, September 1976, 14: 369–88.

Cass, David, and Yaari, Menahem E. "Individual Saving, Aggregate Capital Accumulation, and Efficient Growth." In *Essays on the Theory of Optimal Growth*, edited by Karl Shell. Cambridge, Mass.: MIT Press, 1967.

Darby, Michael R. "The Consumer Expenditure Function." *Explorations in Economic Research*, Winter/Spring 1977-1978, 4: 645–74.

————. *Macroeconomics: The Theory of Income, Employment, and the Price Level.* New York: McGraw-Hill, 1976.

————. "The Permanent Income Theory of Consumption—A Restatement." *Quarterly Journal of Economics*, May 1974, 88: 228–50.

————. "Postwar U.S. Consumption, Consumer Expenditures, and Saving." *American Economic Review, Papers and Proceedings*, May 1975, 65: 217–22.

————. "Review of *The Effect of Social Security on Personal Saving* by Alicia Haydock Munnell." *Journal of Finance*, March 1976, 31: 186–87.

David, Paul A., and Scadding, John L. "Private Savings: Ultrarationality, Aggregation, and 'Dennison's Law.'" *Journal of Political Economy*, March/April 1974, 82: 225–49.

Eisner, Robert. "Capital Shortage: Myth and Reality." *American Economic Review, Papers and Proceedings*, February 1977, 67: 110–15.

Feldstein, Martin. "Does the United States Save Too Little?" *American Economic Review, Papers and Proceedings*, February 1977, 67: 116–21.

————. "Facing the Social Security Crisis." Harvard Institute of Economic Research, Discussion Paper no. 492, July 1976.

————. "Social Security, Induced Retirement, and Aggregate Capital Accumulation." *Journal of Political Economy*, September/October 1974, 82: 905–26.

————. "Social Security and Private Savings: International Evidence in an Extended Life Cycle Model." Harvard Institute of Economic Research, Discussion Paper no. 361, May 1974.

————. "Social Security and Saving: The Extended Life Cycle Theory." *American Economic Review, Papers and Proceedings*, May 1976, 66: 77–86.

Friedman, Milton, and Schwartz, Anna J. *A Monetary History of the United States, 1867–1960.* National Bureau of Economic Research, Studies in Business Cycles 12. Princeton, N.J.: Princeton University Press, 1963.

Ghez, Gilbert R., and Becker, Gary S. *The Allocation of Time and Goods over the Life Cycle.* New York: National Bureau of Economic Research, 1975.

Greville, Thomas N.E. *United States Life Tables and Actuarial Tables 1939–1941.* Washington, D.C.: U.S. Government Printing Office, 1946.

Hanson, James A., and Neher, Phillip A. "The Neoclassical Theorem Once Again: Closed and Open Economies." *American Economic Review*, September 1967, 57: 869–79.

Heckman, James J. "A Life-Cycle Model of Earnings, Learning and Consumption." *Journal of Political Economy*, March/April 1974, 84: S11–S44.

Kendrick, John W. *Productivity Trends in the United States*. National Bureau of Economic Research, General Series 71. Princeton, N.J.: Princeton University Press, 1961.

Kochin, Levis A. "Are Future Taxes Anticipated by Consumers?" *Journal of Money, Credit, and Banking*, August 1974, 6: 385–94.

Kotlikoff, Laurence J., Chamby, Christopher, and Pellechio, Anthony. "Social Security and Private Wealth Accumulation." Unpublished paper. Harvard University, November 1976.

Leijonhufvud, Alex. "Effective Demand Failure." *Swedish Journal of Economics*, 1973, 75: 27–48.

Long, Clarence D. *The Labor Force under Changing Income and Employment*. National Bureau of Economic Research, General Series 65. Princeton, N.J.: Princeton University Press, 1958.

Modigliani, Franco. "The Life Cycle Hypothesis of Saving, the Demand for Wealth, and the Supply of Capital." *Social Research*, June 1966, 33: 160–217.

———, and Brumberg, Richard. "Utility Analysis and the Consumption Function: An Interpretation of Cross-Section Data." In *Post Keynesian Economics*, edited by K. E. Kurihara. New Brunswick, N.J.: Rutgers University Press, 1954.

Munnell, Alicia H. *The Effect of Social Security on Personal Saving*. Cambridge, Mass.: Ballinger Publishing Co., 1974.

———. *The Future of Social Security*. Washington, D.C.: Brookings Institution, 1977.

———. "The Impact of Social Security on Personal Savings." *National Tax Journal*, December 1974, 27: 553–67.

Neher, Phillip A. *Economic Growth and Development: A Mathematical Introduction*. New York: John Wiley and Sons, 1971.

Pechman, Joseph A., Aaron, Henry J., and Taussig, Michael K. *Social Security: Perspectives for Reform*. Washington, D.C.: Brookings Institution, 1968.

Samuelson, Paul A. "An Exact Consumption-Loan Model of Interest with or without the Social Contrivance of Money." *Journal of Political Economy*, December 1958, 66: 467–82.

———. "The Optimal Growth Rate for Population." *International Economic Review*, October 1975, 16: 531–38.

————. "Optimal Social Security in a Life-Cycle Growth Model." *International Economic Review,* October 1975, 16: 539–44.

Smith, James P. "Assets, Savings, and Labor Supply." *Economic Inquiry,* October 1977, 15: 551–73.

Solow, Robert M. *Growth Theory: An Exposition.* Oxford: Oxford University Press, 1970.

Thompson, Earl A. "Debt Instruments in Both Macroeconomic Theory and Capital Theory." *American Economic Review,* December 1967, 57: 1196–1210.

Tobin, James. "Life Cycle Saving and Balanced Growth." In *Ten Economic Studies in the Tradition of Irving Fisher,* by William Fellner and others. New York: John Wiley and Sons, 1967.

LIST OF TABLES AND FIGURES

LIST OF FIGURES